COMPLIANCE AND PUBLIC AUTHORITY

Compliance and Public Authority

A theory with international applications

ORAN R. YOUNG

Published for Resources for the Future
By The Johns Hopkins University Press
Baltimore and London

Copyright © 1979 Resources for the Future, Inc.
Manufactured in the United States of America

Library of Congress Catalog Card Number 79-2193

ISBN 0-8018-2279-3

For Linda

Contents

Preface

The origins of this study lie in some serious doubts I have harbored for many years about several widely shared beliefs pertaining to international relations. Specifically, I have never felt comfortable either with the proposition that the fundamental problems of the international system are attributable to the absence of centralized international institutions of government or with the argument that international law is not really law at all because of the absence of formalized enforcement mechanisms. These doubts have induced me to think repeatedly about the nature of rules in international society as well as about the factors that determine whether individual actors comply with or violate these rules.

Considerations of this sort initiated a thought process that soon led me to broaden my focus. It was not long before I realized that international society is a member of the set of highly decentralized social systems, and that there might well be similarities among all the members of this set with respect to the problem of compliance. From here, it was only natural to take an additional step and to think about the problem of compliance as it arises in the whole class of social systems. As a theoretician, I had little hesitation in expanding the scope of my reflections in search of powerful generalizations about the problem of compliance.

As a result, I quickly found myself engaged in an effort to construct a theory of compliance at the most general level. This effort is reflected in the theoretical chapters of this monograph. Even as I began increasingly to think about compliance in general terms, however, I did not lose interest in the initial puzzles that precipitated my concern. I found that I retained a desire to sort out what struck me as serious confusions about the nature of the international system. Therefore, I have also made a concerted effort to apply my ideas about compliance to that specific case.

As always, it is a pleasure to express my gratitude for the help I have received from a number of institutions and individuals. Among institutions, the Rockefeller Foundation made the crucial contribution by awarding me a fellowship that freed me from teaching duties during the academic year 1975–1976. Resources for the Future added an additional grant that enabled me to finish up the project during 1977. Other institutions that supplied much appreciated logistical support include Tel-Aviv University, The Richardson Institute for Conflict and Peace Research, and the University of Maryland.

Among individuals, I owe a special debt to my good friend, Albert M. Chammah. He not only read the first draft of the manuscript and provided detailed comments, but also participated cheerfully in innumerable discussions dealing with various aspects of compliance. Other colleagues whose assistance has been especially helpful during the course of this study include Michael B. Nicholson, Joe A. Oppenheimer, Clifford S. Russell, and Saadia Touval. I am indebted to my assistant, Robert Warrington, who performed a wide range of tasks for me during the years 1976–1978. My editor, Joan Tron, helped me to eliminate numerous infelicities in the draft of this study. Needless to say, I alone am responsible for all remaining weaknesses and defects in the essay.

O.R.Y.
June 1978

CHAPTER 1

The problem
of compliance

The mere existence of a rule, a law, a moral standard, a social norm, or any other behavioral prescription does not guarantee that those subject to it will actually comply with it. It is evident that various forms of non-compliant behavior are common in most social systems. Even those who acknowledge the authoritativeness and generally favor the existence of specific behavioral prescriptions frequently find it advantageous to violate them in practice.[1] That is, the presence of incentives to cheat need not imply a desire to reject the authoritative force of the relevant behavioral prescriptions altogether. Similarly, the promulgation of a negotiated settlement, a contract, or a treaty does not mean that the participants will automatically conform to the behavioral standards set forth in their agreement. Actors quite frequently enter into agreements whose terms they are by no means determined to carry out.

The issue of compliance invariably poses problems of choice for those who are subject to specific behavioral prescriptions. This is so whether a given actor ultimately chooses to comply or not to comply, either on the basis of conscious calculations or of subconscious forces. Consequently, the phenomenon of compliance is amenable to analysis in terms of various theories of choice. It also constitutes a central concern in all discussions of "enforcement" in the theory of games and in analyses of bargaining and negotiation. Posed in this way, moreover, the problem of compliance comprises a classic theme of political theory. All this leads straight to the principal issues I wish to tackle in this essay. What are the factors that

---

[1] Similarly, Lucy Mair (1962, p. 35) refers to the frequent occurrence of situations in which ". . . the rules to which everyone subscribes in principle are broken in particular cases."

govern whether subjects (individuals or collective entities) abide by rules, laws, moral standards, social norms, agreements, and so forth? How will public authorities approach the problem of compliance and what options do they have in attempting to elicit compliant behavior from specified groups of subjects? These questions encompass a broad range of topics. But, as we shall see, they constitute only a subset of the entire collection of important issues pertaining to behavioral prescriptions and compliance.

I propose to tackle these questions at two distinct levels. In the first instance, I shall address the problem of compliance in general, theoretical terms. Compliance is not uniquely a matter of politics, unless we make it so by definition. On the contrary, issues pertaining to compliance arise in a great many realms. Thus, such issues are pervasive in economic, social, religious, and educational arenas as well as in political arenas more narrowly defined. Furthermore, they constitute a major human concern in situations ranging from highly specific interpersonal relationships to international activities involving large collective entities. Can we formulate any general statements about compliance which are relevant to all these situations? Necessarily, I shall approach the problem in abstract terms in this context and analyze the major features of this problem quite formally.

At the same time, I shall examine the special characteristics of the problem of compliance as it arises in social systems that are highly decentralized with respect to the distribution of power and authority. More specifically, I shall engage in a detailed investigation of compliance in the contemporary international system. In the course of this investigation, I hope to be able to lay to rest certain entrenched myths (for example, the idea that the presence of well-developed enforcement mechanisms constitutes a necessary condition for the achievement of high levels of compliance). Also, I plan to argue that the compliance problems of highly decentralized social systems, like the international system, are not always qualitatively more difficult to solve than the parallel problems arising in more centralized social systems. In this connection, I shall make use of several case studies. I am not, of course, under any illusion that it is possible to confirm generalizations through the use of case materials. Nevertheless, I believe that detailed case studies constitute a flexible device both for the empirical examination of theoretically derived propositions and for the development of new hypotheses within a well-defined conceptual framework.

CONCEPTS AND DEFINITIONS

A behavioral prescription is any well-defined standard setting forth actions (including prohibitions) that members of some specified subject group are expected to perform under appropriate circumstances.[2] A fully

___

[2] According to the dictionary, the term "rule" covers much the same ground that I associate with the concept "behavioral prescription." Thus, *Webster's Collegiate Dic-*

articulated behavioral prescription, therefore, must include a demarcation of the relevant subject group and the appropriate circumstances as well as a statement of the required action(s). Note also that behavioral prescriptions constitute normative standards in the sense that they specify behavior that actors *ought* to exhibit under the circumstances in question.[3] This suggests questions concerning the nature of the authority underlying any given behavioral prescription and the reasons why members of the relevant subject group acknowledge it as authoritative. In this essay, I shall generally bypass these questions by assuming the existence of behavioral prescriptions that are widely acknowledged as authoritative.

The "domain" of a behavioral prescription refers to the subject group encompassed by the prescription. Some prescriptions are intended to be universal (for example, the moral prohibition against the taking of human life) while others are meant only to apply to some well-defined subset of the general population (for example, the rules pertaining to professional baseball). The "scope" of a behavioral prescription, by contrast, refers to the breadth of its coverage. Two dimensions of scope should be differentiated. Some prescriptions require far more extensive or costly actions than others. Thus, moral standards requiring certain individuals to provide substantial and continuous care for others are more extensive than laws demanding periodic performance of marginal acts (for example, having one's automobile inspected annually). Beyond this, however, the term scope applies to contextual limitations associated with behavioral prescriptions or to the appropriate circumstances in which the relevant actions are to be performed. Some prescriptions are broad with respect to scope in the sense that the required actions are to be carried out in virtually every situation (for example, there are relatively few contexts in which the taking of human life is morally or legally justifiable), whereas other prescriptions demand the performance of the appropriate actions only under highly restricted circumstances. Of course, there are also cases in which serious controversies arise precisely with regard to the proper contextual limitations to be associated with a particular behavioral prescription.[4]

A compliance system is a set of behavioral prescriptions designed to regulate an interdependent group of activities in a coherent fashion. Though boundaries are sometimes ambiguous and demarcation problems are common, human activities are typically divisible into relatively well-

---

tionary defines a rule as a prescribed guide for conduct or action. But a number of prominent writers have given the term different meanings in recent philosophical discussions. To avoid confusion with these meanings I have chosen to speak of behavioral prescriptions throughout this monograph. For comparison consider the discussions in Hart (1961, esp. chap. V); Rawls (1955), and Dworkin (1978, esp. chaps. 2 and 3).

[3] Unlike laws of nature or general laws, therefore, behavioral prescriptions may remain valid even in situations where they are frequently violated.

[4] There are parallels between this usage of the concepts "domain" and "scope" and the use of these concepts by Lasswell and Kaplan (1950) in their discussion of power.

defined groups or categories. And behavioral prescriptions are commonly organized into easily differentiable sets to bring order into specific groups of human activities. For example, there are well-developed systems of rules to govern sports like baseball and football; systems of laws to provide order for functional areas such as interstate commerce or regions such as states; and systems of ethics to regulate the behavior of specified groups such as lawyers or physicians. Ideally, a compliance system should be fully consistent internally in the sense that its component prescriptions should not call for contradictory actions or be impossible to fulfill simultaneously. In fact, however, compliance systems exhibit significant inconsistencies from time to time. Note also that there are ordinarily extensive interdependencies among the component elements of compliance systems. Consequently, subjects will often make decisions with respect to the whole set of behavioral prescriptions included in a given compliance system rather than making separate decisions concerning compliance with each component prescription.[5]

The subjects of behavioral prescriptions are the units that must ultimately choose whether or not to comply with any given prescription. In this connection, a subject or an actor is any entity that (1) possesses preferences concerning alternative states of the world and (2) is capable of engaging in choice behavior. An entity that does not possess preferences is not capable of making meaningful choices concerning whether or not to comply with specific behavioral prescriptions. A unit that has no capacity to choose at all must behave in accordance with the dictates of some genuine actor and need not be dealt with separately in any study of compliance.

It is also relevant to touch on the distinction between individuals as actors and collective entities as actors in assessing choice behavior in the realm of compliance. While it is possible to proceed on the assumption that collective entities behave as though they were integrated individuals, their actual choice behavior diverges significantly from that of individuals in many real-world situations. This is particularly true with respect to the behavior of the actors in the international system, a case of special interest in the context of this study (Allison, 1971). Accordingly, it will be important to engage in a careful examination of the nature of the actors and their behavioral attributes in analyzing the problem of compliance as it arises in the international system.

The term compliance refers to all behavior by subjects or actors that conforms to the requirements of behavioral prescriptions or compliance systems. Conversely, noncompliance (or violation) is behavior that fails

---

[5] For example, when you agree to participate in a particular game, you ordinarily accept the entire set of rules of the game in question. Similarly, if you agree to operate within the framework of an existing parliamentary system, you generally accept the rules of that system as a set.

to conform to such requirements.[6] In general, compliance or noncompliance with any specific behavioral prescription by a given actor involves an act of choice. However, such behavior may sometimes become largely habitual or subconscious, so that it is not necessary to assume that actors always engage in extensive calculations concerning such problems.[7]

A compliance mechanism is any institution or set of institutions (formal or informal) established by a public authority (for example, a government in a centralized social system or a diplomatic conference or *ad hoc* functional agency in a highly decentralized social system)[8] for the purpose of encouraging compliance with one or more behavioral prescriptions of a compliance system. Compliance mechanisms obviously give rise to efforts to structure the incentives of the members of specified subject groups with respect to their choices concerning compliant and noncompliant behavior. One way to do this is through direct interventions in the decision making processes of subjects. Interventions of this type may take such varied forms as: (1) punishments or rewards,[9] (2) inspection systems operating to reduce the probability of subjects engaging in undetected violations, and (3) the keeping of public records so that subjects violating prescriptions will subsequently be burdened with records of noncompliant behavior. On the other hand, compliance mechanisms sometimes rely on efforts to mold the underlying criteria of evaluation that actors use in their decision making about compliance. For example, public authorities can invest resources in programs of socialization designed to inculcate such things as habits of obedience or internalized norms.[10]

Public authorities will typically face a multiplicity of investment decisions concerning the use of resources for the development and operation of compliance mechanisms. Not only is there the basic decision about the proportion of the overall budget to devote to them as opposed to other goods, there is also the question of what mix of mechanisms will prove

[6] Throughout this essay, I use the term compliance rather than the term obedience. I look upon compliance as a response to a generalized behavioral prescription as it applies to a specific situation. Thus, a given actor decides whether to comply with or violate a particular rule, law, or social norm under the circumstances at hand. By contrast, I regard obedience as a response to a command from an identifiable authority figure in a specific situation. Here one actor commands another to do something (or to refrain from doing something) and the target actor decides whether to obey or to defy the command.

[7] In this connection, see also Hart's (1961, chap. IV) discussion of the "habit of obedience."

[8] There is a tendency to equate the category of public authorities with formal institutions of government. In fact, governments constitute an important special case of the broader category of public authorities. But the category also encompasses a variety of other institutional arrangements (both formal and informal). Therefore, it is meaningful to speak of public authorities in the context of highly decentralized social systems.

[9] Much of the formal work on compliance emphasizes this segment of the broader problem (Becker, 1968 and Stigler, 1970).

[10] To date, the literature on socialization has seldom dealt explicitly with the links between socialization and decision making.

optimal in dealing with the set of compliance problems considered likely to arise during the foreseeable future. Public authorities will ordinarily have to make a stream of decisions in this realm based on considerations relating to such matters as production functions, fixed costs versus operating costs, problems of lumpiness, and the impact of changing technology. At this point, I wish only to flag the importance of these issues; I shall have more to say about them in a subsequent chapter.

PRINCIPAL QUESTIONS

The principal questions pursued in this study fall quite naturally under a small number of headings. Though each of these headings encompasses a range of topics, it is possible to characterize them with some precision.

The calculus of the individual actor

It is apparent that individuals in most social systems make continuous streams of choices concerning compliance and noncompliance. The typical actor is a member of numerous subject groups toward which behavioral prescriptions of various types are directed. Empirically, it is clear that choices both to comply and to violate occur with considerable frequency in conjunction with most behavioral prescriptions (Rottenberg, 1973). But is it possible to model these choices in such a way as to be able to explain or predict the behavior of individual actors in various situations?[11]

At the outset, we need to identify the factors that go into the calculations of subjects concerning the benefits and costs of compliance. This leads to a range of more specific questions such as the following. How do actors cope with cross-pressures when specific prescriptions conflict with one another? To what extent do actors generate and use expectations concerning the probable behavior of others in making their own decisions? How do subjects react to probabilistic sanctions in making choices?[12] Are there significant differences in the ways in which actors respond to rewards and punishments in their calculations? Do actors develop decision rules or habitual responses to simplify choices, in view of the fact that there are numerous choices of this type to be made in each time period and that such choices will often be iterative in nature?

Perhaps the most elegant way to proceed with theory construction in this area would be to develop a generalized utility function incorporating all the factors (that is, benefits and costs) the individual subject considers in making choices regarding compliance.[13] In principle, this would permit the application of marginal analysis and the calculation of equilibrium

[11] For surveys of relevant theoretical work on choice consult, *inter alia,* Simon (1959) and Edwards and Tversky (1967).

[12] Note also that the relevant probabilities will often be subjective rather than objective. On the significance of this distinction see Rapoport (1964).

[13] For an interesting and important attempt to proceed in this fashion consult Becker (1968).

conditions for subjects with respect to compliance and noncompliance. However, I do not believe this approach will prove fruitful. These choices are ordinarily so deeply affected by indivisibilities, uncertainty, strategic interaction, complex nonmonetary payoffs, and competition from other choice problems that models based on elaborate utility equations for individual actors will be empirically inapplicable and will often become a source of confusion. Instead, I would argue that successful analyses of choice behavior in this realm will require careful attention to such things as decision rules subjects employ in coping with uncertainty, subjective estimates they use to deal with strategic interaction, and policies they develop to handle classes or types of compliance choices that crop up repeatedly over time.[14]

The behavior of public authorities

Whatever their behavioral attributes or institutional characteristics, public authorities will always face opportunity costs with respect to the investment of resources in compliance mechanisms, since the total pool of available resources is finite and there are many other demands on it. Accordingly, they will be interested in cutting compliance costs, particularly if this can be done without precipitating large upswings in the level of violations. The pervasiveness of uncertainty and the fact that public authorities are generally better situated to manipulate information than individual subjects will make it possible to cut corners on compliance mechanisms in some cases. Nevertheless, public authorities must reckon with the fact that compliance decisions by subjects will often be influenced by strategic interaction, so that extreme efforts to economize on compliance mechanisms will invite the emergence of coordinated activities among actors interested in initiating a rebellion or achieving fundamental changes in the prevailing behavioral prescriptions.[15]

This perspective stimulates a variety of questions. How much is it rational for a public authority to invest in specific institutions (formal or informal) designed to elicit compliant behavior from particular groups of subjects? What do public authorities generally try to maximize, and what are the resultant implications for the efforts of such authorities to encourage compliant behavior?[16] What types of compliance mechanisms are most "efficient," and does the answer to this question vary from one functional area to another? Are there complementarities among analytically separable compliance problems so that it is possible to achieve economies of scale by constructing a small number of large compliance mechanisms rather

[14] For a related discussion of decision rules see Tversky and Kahneman (1974).

[15] For an extended discussion of the phenomenon of strategic interaction see Young (1975).

[16] That is, what sort of role premise do public authorities have? On the concept "role premise" see Scitovsky (1943).

than a large number of small ones? To what extent does prevailing technology affect the productivity of investments in compliance mechanisms, and is it rational to engage in extensive research and development in an effort to achieve technological innovations that will increase the efficiency of compliance mechanisms? Are there special types of compliance mechanisms that are particularly appropriate for use in highly decentralized or anarchical social systems such as the international system? To what extent is it possible to engage successfully in social engineering with respect to the design of optimal compliance mechanisms for use in specific contexts?

There are various ways to proceed in efforts to answer questions of this sort. My initial hypothesis, however, is that public authorities make extensive use of aggregate assumptions in this realm rather than emphasizing microlevel interactions with specific subjects which will inevitably be deeply affected by strategic interaction (Frohlich, Oppenheimer, and Young, 1971). For example, I am convinced that governments generally use aggregate assumptions about such things as the marginal productivity of additional expenditures on various types of compliance mechanisms and the marginal social costs of specified increases in the level of violations allowed to occur in the relevant social system.[17] In this connection, I would argue that appropriate models for the analysis of the behavior of public authorities in this realm should employ aggregate assumptions similar to the assumptions used by the authorities themselves.

Externalities of compliance mechanisms

There is every reason to expect that the development and operation of compliance mechanisms in a social system will generate externalities, in the sense of unintended by-products of actions designed to elicit compliance.[18] These externalities may sometimes be valued positively. It may prove possible, for example, to make use of the institutions created to deal with compliance problems to supply positively valued collective goods such as a sense of community or a general atmosphere of trust (Frohlich, Oppenheimer, and Young, 1971, chapter 2). On the other hand, there will be cases in which compliance mechanisms are capable of generating negative externalities of major proportions. To take an obvious illustration, authoritarian leaders may use information gathered by compliance mechanisms for legitimate purposes in ways that lead to far-reaching inroads on fundamental civil liberties. My primary concern with the externalities of compliance mechanisms will center on this danger of severe negative by-products.

This basic perspective generates the following sorts of questions. Are some types of compliance mechanisms apt to be more conducive to the

---

[17] This usage of the concept "social cost" is spelled out in chapter 6.

[18] Technically, an externality is a by-product of some action undertaken for other purposes, the value of which is not reflected by any market mechanism. For a variety of theoretical perspectives on externalities consult Staaf and Tannian (1973).

production of negative externalities than others? What normative standards regarding externalities should be taken into account in the construction and operation of compliance mechanisms? In cases of conflict, what trade-offs are we prepared to accept between the achievement of compliance on the one hand and the preservation of such things as civil liberties on the other? Are there safety devices that can be built into compliance mechanisms at a reasonable cost and that will serve to minimize the dangers of negative externalities associated with such mechanisms? To what extent does the use of certain technologies in the realm of compliance (for example, technologies of inspection and surveillance) encourage the emergence of negative externalities quite apart from the conscious intentions of specific authorities or leaders?

The principal issues I wish to examine in this area have an explicit normative component. Specifically, I propose to discuss various normative standards that seem to me appropriate in regulating the uses of compliance mechanisms, and I intend to assess the range of feasible trade-offs between efficiency in eliciting compliant behavior and the maintenance of standards dealing with such things as the preservation of basic civil liberties. Furthermore, I plan to pursue the issue of developing safeguards that will permit the minimization of negative externalities without interfering unduly with the achievement of compliance in various functional areas.[19]

THE BROADER SETTING

The problem of compliance, as I have described it, should be placed in a broader setting. The formulation I have outlined is certainly not the only possible one.[20] By way of illustration, some may object to my demarcation of the category of behavioral prescriptions, and others may have difficulties with the whole idea of conceptualizing the problem of compliance in terms of choice behavior. Moreover, though I have indicated an interest in a broad range of questions pertaining to compliance, there are important related issues with which I do not intend to grapple in this essay. In this section, then, I wish to differentiate the problem of compliance as I shall approach it from a number of related issues.

In the first instance, I want to contrast my point of view with the contractarian perspective articulated recently by Rawls (1971). Rawls is fundamentally interested in the identification of a set of general principles or behavioral prescriptions that all rational individuals would agree to in what he calls the "original position." In this connection, he draws a distinction between "ideal theory" and "partial compliance theory." In the

---

[19] These questions are somewhat out of the mainstream of contemporary theoretical work dealing with externalities. For the most part, the mainstream of work in this area is well represented by the essays collected in Staaf and Tannian (1973).

[20] See, for example, the essays in Pennock and Chapman (1970). I find especially interesting the formulation offered by Stuart S. Nagel, "Causes and Effects of Constitutional Compliance," pp. 219–229.

case of ideal theory, individuals ". . . assume that the principles they acknowledge, whatever they are, will be strictly complied with and followed by everyone." Partial compliance theory, by contrast, deals with situations in which principles or behavioral prescriptions are sometimes violated even by those who acknowledge their validity.[21] In his contractarian analysis, Rawls focuses on the case of ideal theory and proceeds with the effort to identify a set of preferred principles without reference to the problem of compliance. In my analysis, on the other hand, I begin with the premise that partial compliance theory encompasses the bulk of interesting real-world situations and proceed to focus my analysis on the problem of compliance itself. Among other things, this leads to an interest in the identification of "efficient" principles or behavioral prescriptions rather than those that would be preferred under an assumption of perfect compliance.

I also want to distinguish my focus of attention from the issues of *recognition* and *validity* considered by Hart (1961, chap. VI) in his analysis of rules. In essence, the question of recognition is a demarcation problem concerning the criteria to be used in distinguishing between assertions that are genuine rules in a given social system and assertions that are not actually rules. Similarly, the closely related issue of validity concerns the acceptability or legitimacy of rules. As Hart himself puts it (1961, p. 100), "To say that a given rule is valid is to recognize it as passing all the tests provided by the rule of recognition and so as a rule of the system." There is no doubt that the questions of recognition and validity are important in conjunction with what I call behavioral prescriptions, just as they are in the context of Hart's rules. They go directly to the problem of testing for the existence of behavioral prescriptions, and they raise some initial questions concerning what Hart (1961, pp. 97–107) calls the "internal" perspective on rules. But these are not the central questions I have chosen to pursue in this essay.

Yet another tack that I do not take in this essay concerns the welfare implications of differentiable sets of behavioral prescriptions (Buchanan and Tullock, 1962). Not only is it possible to imagine the promulgation of alternative sets of such prescriptions in most social systems, it is also apparent that these sets of prescriptions generally will not be neutral with respect to their welfare implications. That is, actors will typically stand to gain or lose depending upon the particular set of prescriptions introduced to govern their behavior. Under the circumstances, it is interesting to compare sets of prescriptions to determine how they would affect the welfare of the individuals in a social system and to analyze the allocative mechanisms built into each set. Beyond this, the existence of alternative sets of behavioral prescriptions will have implications pertaining to *social*

---

[21] Both the quote and the characterization of partial compliance theory are from Rawls (1971, p. 351).

welfare in any given social system (Rothenberg, 1961). Perhaps the best known criterion of evaluation in this context is the standard of Pareto optimality. Does the introduction of a set of behavioral prescriptions in a system previously characterized by their absence constitute a Pareto optimal move in the sense that it improves the position of some actors without damaging the position of any actor?[22] Is it possible to identify some sets of behavioral prescriptions that are Pareto superior to others in the context of a given social system? While all these issues are intrinsically important, they are not the ones I have chosen to focus on in this essay. Thus, I start with situations in which some set of behavioral prescriptions exists for better or for worse. In this connection, I emphasize the choices of subjects concerning whether or not to comply with these prescriptions and the investment decisions of public authorities with respect to the development of compliance mechanisms.

Finally, it is clear that there are important questions concerning the dynamics of behavioral prescriptions in all social systems. How do prescriptions and compliance systems come into existence and how do they change over time? These are questions that have been widely discussed under such headings as law creation and the sources of law.[23] They are, at the heart of the classic controversies among natural law theorists, legal positivists, and legal realists (Goulding, 1966). Questions of this type are also approachable in terms of the modern theory of collective or public goods (Olson, 1965 and Frohlich, Oppenheimer, and Young, 1971). This is so because compliance systems (or alterations in such systems) take the form of relatively pure collective goods in most social systems. Among other things, this suggests that behavioral prescriptions and compliance systems will be difficult to supply in many social systems and that there will generally be a tendency toward underinvestment in this realm. Important as they are, however, these issues also do not lie at the heart of my concerns in this essay. I am concerned above all with the problem of compliance with existing behavioral prescriptions.

In short, though the issues I pursue in this essay are broad ones, they are relatively well defined and they certainly do not encompass all the intrinsically interesting questions pertaining to behavioral prescriptions and compliance. Briefly, I start from the observation that some set of behavioral prescriptions is ordinarily operative in a social system at any given moment.[24] I assume that individual actors make steady streams of

[22] It is widely believed that the introduction of some set of behavioral prescriptions constitutes a necessary (though perhaps not sufficient) condition for individual survival in group situations. In a sense, this is the central insight of all contractarian thinking.

[23] It is possible to obtain a number of insights in this realm by examining the contrasting views presented in Hart (1961) and Fuller (1964).

[24] Social systems may of course go through periods of disruption and change with respect to their behavioral prescriptions. Nevertheless, the assertion in the text seems reasonable as a broad generalization.

choices (conscious or subconscious) concerning compliance with these prescriptions. I further assume that the decision processes of individual actors are sufficiently regular to support a search for falsifiable generalizations relating to the problem of compliance. In addition, I focus on both the empirical and the normative dimensions of the behavior of public authorities as they make decisions about the investment of resources in institutions designed to encourage compliant behavior by specified groups of subjects.

PART I

A special theory of compliance

CHAPTER 2

The calculus
of the actor

Suppose you find yourself having to decide whether to comply with or to violate some well-defined behavioral prescription. Imagine, for example, that you are trying to decide whether to report a certain type of nonsalary income on your tax return. Or you are a student wondering whether to seek impermissible help on a take-home examination. Or you are an individual endeavoring to sell an automobile and considering whether to fabricate information concerning the true condition of the vehicle. How do you go about making decisions concerning such matters? Do you make a conscious effort to weigh the costs and benefits associated with compliance and with violation? If so, what factors do you take into account and how do you weight them?

As these examples suggest, I propose to treat the problem of compliance with behavioral prescriptions as a matter of choice by the individual actor or subject. Several clarifying comments are in order at the outset. A choice occurs whenever an actor selects a specific alternative from a set of two or more alternatives.[1] This implies that subjects are able to discern differentiated alternatives in their environments, to formulate preferences among these alternatives, and to employ some criterion or decision rule to select a given alternative in a specific situation.[2] But this assumption does not

---

[1] A helpful collection of theoretical works relating to choice is Page (1968).

[2] "Rational" choice is a subset of the broader category of choice behavior. That is, actors can make choices without doing so in a rational fashion. In general, the concept of rational choice refers to choice behavior that is conscious and purposive. But these attributes are not sufficient to identify the category of rational choice with precision. More specifically, then, rational choice is the choice behavior of actors that (1) formulate transitive preferences over sets of alternatives, (2) exhibit stable preferences across given alternative sets so long as their information remains unchanged, and (3) always select their most preferred alternative. For a good survey consult Riker and Ordeshook (1973).

prejudge two other issues. It is possible for subjects to make choices even if they do not consciously or systematically weigh the costs and benefits of specific alternatives. In addition, subjects may group similar choice problems together and formulate general policies relating to such groups, so that it is not necessary to make fresh calculations as new cases arise which fit into well-defined categories. I shall have more to say about the relevance of these issues to the problem of compliance later.[3]

THE BEHAVIOR OF INDIVIDUAL SUBJECTS

My purpose in this section is to make explicit the basic postulates about the behavior of individual actors or subjects of behavioral prescriptions which I employ throughout the essay. Two general comments seem pertinent. I do *not* make use of some of the behavioral assumptions that are central to many formal theories of choice. For example, I do not believe that subjects are capable of computing numerical utilities or constructing formal utility functions in making choices about compliance.[4] The implications of this position will become apparent as I proceed with my analysis. Beyond this, I am convinced that it is desirable to specify a somewhat different set of behavioral assumptions for subjects than for public authorities in analyzing the problem of compliance. The precise differences I find useful will become clear from a comparison of the argument of this chapter with the analysis of behavior of public authorities in chapter 7.

Let me turn now to some specific assumptions about the behavior of individual subjects:

1. Subjects are decision makers in the sense that they make continuous streams of choices among alternatives. This is so whether any given choice is made consciously or unconsciously.[5]

2. Individual subjects confront a multiplicity of choice problems in the same general time period, but decision-making capacity is always limited.

[3] Note also that it is not necessary to begin by conceptualizing the problem of compliance as a matter of choice. For example, it would be possible to approach the behavior of individual subjects with respect to compliance or violation in terms of the ideas associated with psychological conditioning or behavior modification. Alternatively, one might proceed in a highly inductive fashion to seek out empirical correlates of compliance and violation. This would lead to analyses of the extent to which compliant behavior is positively or negatively associated with such things as education, occupation, income, and so forth. It is evident that efforts to approach the problem of compliance along these lines would differ fundamentally from my efforts to approach the problem as a matter of choice on the part of individual actors or subjects. I emphasize this distinction not because I want to claim that my approach is intrinsically superior or ontologically correct. Rather, I want to place my own approach to the problem of compliance in perspective and to minimize confusion concerning the underlying conceptual structure of this study.

[4] Nor do I think that it makes sense to assume that subjects behave *as if* they could compute numerical utilities in this realm. For a collection of essays dealing with the assumptions characteristic of formal theories of choice see Edwards and Tversky (1967).

[5] Fundamentally, then, my starting point is similar to that of neoclassical microeconomics. In this connection, see also Henderson and Quandt (1958).

Therefore, subjects will be unable to devote their undivided attention to specific choice problems, and they will experience continuous pressures to minimize the attention devoted to any particular problem. At the same time, subjects will not regard all the choice problems they face at any given time as equally important. They will attempt, at least crudely, to rank these problems in terms of importance to themselves, and they will allocate their attention on the basis of this rank ordering. This implies that conscious decision making will be more common with respect to choice problems which individual actors regard as important and that general policies will be utilized most commonly to dispose of less important choice problems.

3. In making compliance choices, individual subjects will act to maximize their own welfare. That is, they will compute costs and benefits in the realm of compliance on the basis of self-interest, without regard to the welfare of others as an end in itself (Frohlich, 1974).

4. Subjects will think in terms of the *expected value* of alternatives in the realm of compliance (Rapoport, 1964: Part 1). In this connection, they will often find it necessary to employ subjective probabilities, and the payoffs associated with various possible outcomes will sometimes be difficult to specify with precision.[6] But they will exhibit a lively interest in the probabilities associated with outcomes as well as with the outcomes themselves.

5. Subjects will endeavor to maximize the *present* value of their choices by employing some sort of time discount. That is, future costs and benefits will be multiplied by some fraction less than 1 for inclusion in present value calculations. I do not assume, however, that subjects possess identical discount rates.[7]

6. The subject groups for some behavioral prescriptions will include collective entities as well as (or instead of) individuals. In real-world situations, behavioral prescriptions are often directed toward such collective entities as corporations, labor unions, interest groups, political parties, and states. I shall have much more to say about the choice behavior of collective entities in chapter 3. Here I will only state that I do not find it absurd to assume that collective entities develop preferences among alternatives in the realm of compliance. The processes through which they arrive at preferences are typically complex, and in some cases the preference orderings may be neither transitive nor stable.[8] But these observations in no way suggest that collective entities do not make choices in the

[6] On these complications see Daniel Ellsberg, "The Theory and Practice of Blackmail," in Young (1975, pp. 343–363).

[7] I think it is reasonable to assume that all subjects will experience decreasing marginal costs and benefits as a function of time. But the exact form of this relationship will vary from subject to subject.

[8] It is evident, for example, that collective choices arrived at through processes of voting or bargaining will not always be transitive or stable.

realm of compliance or that they fail to develop preferences pertaining to the relevant alternatives.

BASES OF COMPLIANCE

Given this conception of individual behavior, the next step is to identify and examine the incentives of subjects as they make choices about compliance and violation. It is apparent that there are several types of incentives and that they need not be mutually exclusive.

Self-interest

Even when there are no public authorities and social pressures are absent, individual subjects may conclude that the expected value of compliance outweighs that of violation. In other words, compliance will sometimes emerge as a preferred option in purely utilitarian terms, even in the absence of any external sanctions or social pressures. This is one reason why analyses of compliance that treat enforcement as a necessary condition for the achievement of compliant behavior convey a distorted picture.

It is possible to distinguish several types of situations in which compliance will be chosen over violation on the basis of simple self-interest calculations.[9] Thus, I may impose on myself explicit prescriptions in order to ensure that I get enough exercise, adhere to a balanced diet, or maintain a desired work schedule. Similarly, I may voluntarily comply with certain externally articulated prescriptions, such as rules requiring me to undergo periodic physical examinations or to discard bald tires on my automobile.

Considerations of reciprocity can also produce situations in which compliance is preferred to violation on the basis of self-interest calculations.[10] A subject facing a particular compliance problem may conclude that others will be more likely to comply if he complies and more likely to violate if he violates. Or he may conclude that the best decision rule for himself is to behave toward others as he would prefer them to behave toward himself. In either case, to the extent that the subject prefers a world in which everyone complies with a particular prescription to one in which they all violate it, he will conclude that his own preferred course of action is to comply. There is considerable evidence to suggest that calculations of this general sort constitute a critical basis of compliance in many areas, from highly restricted interpersonal interactions to international relations (Gergen, 1969).

[9] I use the term "self-interest" here to refer to behavior based on utilitarian calculations of costs and benefits in the absence of any external sanctions or social pressures. Note that this use of the term is not identical to the meaning attached to self-interest earlier in this chapter in the discussion of behavioral assumptions. So long as this distinction is borne in mind, it should not cause serious problems.

[10] For discussions of legal prescriptions that emphasize the notion of reciprocity heavily see Malinowski (1926) and Hoebel (1954).

Consider next the case of a subject who wishes to engage in beneficial relations with numerous other actors during the same general time period. His ability to develop favorable relations with any particular partner will ordinarily depend on the maintenance of a reputation for complying with certain basic rules in his dealings with others. This will be especially true whenever it is difficult to prevent the dissemination of information about such matters within the relevant social system. In such cases, incentives to comply with prescriptions will frequently be decisive even if violation seems tempting in the context of individual interactions. A variation on this theme concerns what may be described as the discipline of time. This phenomenon arises when the same actors engage in iterative or quasi-iterative interactions over time. Here a prior record of compliance with certain rules or adherence to agreements will often be critical to the ability of an actor to obtain favorable results in subsequent interactions. Under the circumstances, pure self-interest will suggest the importance of establishing a record of compliant behavior in at least a reasonable proportion of cases in the series. Moreover, a past violation by an actor may serve as a precedent for other actors who wish to engage in violations. Accordingly, an actor will have a distinct incentive to avoid contributing to precedents for violations that may damage him.[11]

Beyond this, individual subjects will have a definite interest in the continued viability of various compliance systems in their social environment.[12] To the extent that their own violations appear to weaken whole compliance systems, therefore, subjects may conclude that the costs to them of violation (even in present value terms) will exceed any costs associated with compliance in specific instances. This type of incentive depends, of course, on the subject's estimate of the likelihood that his behavior will make a difference with respect to the maintenance of some larger compliance system.[13] A variety of factors will affect such estimates in specific situations. For example, there is little doubt that subjects will be more likely to think of their own behavior as making a difference in small groups than in large groups.[14] Similarly, subjects who occupy positions as opinion leaders may be more susceptible to considerations of this type than sub-

[11] For further discussion of such phenomena as precedents and reputation consult Schelling (1960).

[12] That is, the absence of rules or behavioral prescriptions will constitute a Pareto inferior situation in virtually all social systems.

[13] This type of reasoning is analogous to some of the broader considerations introduced by students of voting to account for voting by individuals who might be expected to abstain on the basis of narrower considerations. For an exposition and critique of the relevant analyses of voting see Barry (1970).

[14] Another way to look at this problem is to think of the continued viability of any given compliance system as a collective good within the relevant group. In this connection, there is general agreement on the proposition that it is easier to induce individuals to contribute toward the supply of collective goods in small groups than in large groups (Olson, 1965).

jects who do not regard themselves as prominent and who believe that their own violations will go largely unnoticed. Nevertheless, there is every reason to believe that this form of self-interest will sometimes play a substantial role in inducing subjects to comply with behavioral prescriptions.

Enforcement

While it would be a mistake to underestimate the power of self-interest as a basis of compliance, there can be no doubt that subjects are also sensitive to the deliberate use of sanctions by public authorities to enforce compliance (Reisman, 1971). Enforcement involves explicit attempts by the authority to manipulate the cost-benefit calculations of subjects. When sanctions are actually applied, I shall speak of punishment as a form of enforcement; when they are merely threatened, I shall refer to the use of threats to achieve compliance.

The basic premise underlying enforcement is that compliance can be obtained efficiently by making violation unattractive rather than by altering the costs or benefits of compliance. Therefore, it is important to identify the variables that the subject will take into account in computing the expected value of violation.[15] These variables will include: the probability of violating without being detected, the benefits associated with undetected violations, the probability of being detected but escaping explicit sanctions, the payoff flowing from this outcome, the probability of being detected and sanctioned, and the costs of the relevant sanctions. Having aggregated these factors in some fashion, the subject will compare the expected value of violation with the expected value of compliance, and he will choose compliance if the latter exceeds the former. The public authority can concentrate its efforts on minimizing the chances of violations going undetected, maximizing the probability that sanctions will follow the detection of violations, or making sanctions large (Stigler, 1970). Or it can try some combination of these activities. Many policy debates relating to compliance focus precisely on the specification of emphases among these alternative activities.

Several empirical observations pertaining to enforcement seem appropriate at this point. It is well known that the expected costs of violation are low in many real-world situations. With respect to certain types of crime, for example, a high proportion of violations ultimately go undetected, and even those people whose violations are detected often find it possible to escape the force of sanctions.[16] This does not mean, however, that enforcement efforts on the part of public authorities will be inefficacious. Much depends on the costs and benefits associated with compliance in specific cases as well as on the expected value of violation. In some cases, making violation only slightly less attractive could tip the balance in favor of compliance.

---

[15] A more formal analysis of these conditions appears in Becker (1968).
[16] For empirical evidence consult the essays in Rottenberg (1973).

There has been some debate concerning the relative importance of the major variables in the calculations of potential violators. In the recent literature on crime, for example, the probability of being sanctioned is generally stressed as being more important than the size or magnitude of the sanctions (Becker, 1968 and Tullock, 1974). Should this finding prove valid in other contexts, it would suggest that low probability sanctions, which are perfectly feasible in principle, do not constitute an attractive policy option for public authorities.[17]

Inducement

Public authorities often attempt to elicit compliance through the use of inducement. Like enforcement, inducement involves attempts on the part of some well-defined external actor to manipulate the cost-benefit calculations of subjects. Inducements can take the form of actual rewards or only promises.

In contrast to enforcement, the premise underlying inducement is that it is often more efficient to raise the expected value of compliance rather than to reduce the expected value of violation. The central decision variables in the realm of inducement are: the probability that the subject's compliant behavior will be identified and rewarded, the nature of the reward in this case, the probability that compliance will be detected but not explicitly rewarded, the payoff to the subject under this condition, the probability that compliance will go undetected, and the results for the subject of this outcome. In this case, the subject will compute the expected value of compliance and compare it with some measure of the expected value of violation. If the former outweighs the latter, he will choose the path of compliance. This suggests that public authorities utilizing inducement can focus on efforts to increase the size of rewards, raise the probability that detected compliance will be rewarded, or reduce the chances of compliance going undetected. And of course such authorities may attempt to employ some combination of these measures.

If there is a definite parallel between inducement and enforcement, it may be that the probability of being rewarded is more critical to the choices of subjects than the nature of the reward itself. This would suggest that a strong emphasis on low probability rewards, which are perfectly feasible in principle, would not make sense for public authorities. It is not self-evident, however, that this parallel is fully valid, and it seems clear that more work is needed on this issue. Next, there is an important asymmetry between enforcement and inducement from the point of view of public authorities. Enforcement is particularly costly to them when it

[17] This line of reasoning raises fundamental doubts about the policy of nuclear deterrence, which has served as the foundation of American strategic thinking during most of the postwar period. Nevertheless, the issues are complex. Some students of deterrence have suggested that there are significant interaction effects between the probability of punishment and the severity of punishment, so that it is not possible to weigh the relative importance of these factors in a straightforward fashion.

fails to elicit compliant behavior from the relevant group of subjects, whereas inducement is particularly costly when it does elicit compliant behavior (Baldwin, 1971). This is so because punishments must be meted out in the wake of violations while rewards must be distributed when subjects actually comply. Paradoxically, this suggests that a public authority confidently expecting to succeed in its efforts to obtain compliance is more likely to rely heavily upon enforcement than one possessing a lower sense of efficacy. Beyond this, enforcement and inducement are not mutually exclusive in most situations. It is generally possible for public authorities to pursue "carrot and stick" policies. In fact, policy debates relating to compliance frequently turn on arguments concerning the appropriate mix of enforcement and inducement to employ rather than on claims advocating the exclusive use of one or the other (Frohlich and Oppenheimer, 1974).

Social pressure

The actions of public authorities do not exhaust the range of external factors that subjects take into account in making decisions about compliance. Subjects may have incentives to comply with behavioral prescriptions which stem from their sensitivity or responsiveness to the evaluations of other actors even though these other actors do not have the status of public authorities (Cartwright and Zander, 1968 and Kiesler and Kiesler, 1969). Peer group pressures in such areas as dress codes and linguistic conventions constitute clear-cut examples of this phenomenon, but it would be easy to identify numerous illustrations in other realms.

In most situations, social pressure can take both negative and positive forms. Negative pressures include: ostracism or expulsion from a given group, avoidance, lack of trust, and the dissemination of negative opinions about a particular subject. Positive pressures, on the other hand, typically encompass such things as social approval, the extension of status, and offers of friendship. As with other external incentives, probabilities are important in the realm of social pressure. That is, subjects will be concerned not only with types of social pressure but also with the probability of experiencing it. To the best of my knowledge, however, it is not possible to say much at this time about the relative importance of probabilities in this realm. In some cases, a small probability that a certain form of behavior will be publicized is sufficient to deter a subject, while there are other situations in which subjects are willing brazenly to ignore the evaluations of other actors.

The impact of social pressures on compliance decisions may vary along several dimensions. There are undoubtedly variations across cultures in the extent to which social pressure plays a role in eliciting compliance. Even within the same culture, some individuals will be less sensitive than others to the evaluative reactions of outsiders. This is one of the things conveyed by the distinction between "inner directed" and "other directed" behavior (Riesman, 1950). A given subject may also be intensely concerned about the reactions of a certain well-defined group of outsiders but care little about the reactions of others. Similarly, subjects will often be sensitive to the reactions of different reference groups in different realms of behavior. For example, I may react to the evaluations of one reference group with respect to my professional activities and to the reactions of another group when it comes to my performance in personal relationships. All this suggests that the impact of social pressures on decisions about compliance will exhibit complex patterns in most real-world situations.

Obligation

So far, I have been analyzing the incentives for compliance in purely utilitarian terms. But subjects are undoubtedly influenced by nonutilitarian considerations in many situations. The term "obligation" encompasses incentives to comply with behavioral prescriptions which stem from a general sense of duty and which do not rest on explicit calculations of costs and benefits. For example, a subject may feel an obligation to tell the truth or to comply with laws requiring full disclosure, regardless of the consequences.

The nature of obligations is a theme that has occupied the attention of many political philosophers. To comply with the rules of a sovereign or with valid laws out of a sense of duty is surely different from complying because the expected value of compliance outweighs the expected value of violation in a given situation. But what is the ultimate normative source of an obligation to comply with a given behavioral prescription?[18] In the end, this question must lead either to an infinite regress or to the formulation of some metaphysical first principle. Intellectually, neither of these outcomes is entirely satisfactory. Despite these analytic difficulties, feelings of obligation can constitute a powerful incentive to comply with behavioral prescriptions in specific situations.

In fact, there is some reason to believe that feelings of obligation often play a significant role in compliance choices.[19] This suggests the importance of examining the social psychological bases of obligation in contrast to the philosophical status of the concept. How do individuals acquire obligations? Is the importance attached to obligations related to identifiable personality variables? What is the role of socialization in the development of feelings of obligation? (Bronfenbrenner, 1970). Are there substantial

[18] For a selection of views on this subject see Pennock and Chapman (1970). For a particularly acute discussion of this problem consult Pitkin (1965) and Pitkin (1966).
[19] On the distinction between feeling an obligation and feeling obliged see Hart (1961, pp. 79–88). In essence, the distinction rests on the difference between acting out of inner conviction and acting in response to external pressures. One may feel obliged to do something because of the force of external sanctions or social pressures. One feels an obligation to do something in order to avoid violating one's own convictions.

variations across cultures in the extent to which obligation is stressed as a basis of compliance? Are subjects more likely to experience feelings of obligation toward systems of prescriptions as such or toward the prescriptions articulated by some designated authority regardless of their content? Are subjects able to make clear-cut functional distinctions between prescriptions with which they feel an obligation to comply and those they feel they can view in terms of concrete costs and benefits? If I am right in suggesting that obligation plays a significant role in the thinking of many subjects about compliance, each of these questions will require investigation in some depth.

Habit or practice

Finally, it is is important to recognize that the decisions of subjects concerning compliance are often influenced by subconscious or unconscious considerations. I use the terms "habit" and "practice" to refer to patterns of behavior, acquired by frequent repetition, which manifest themselves in regularity of performance. A subject complies habitually when he simply conforms to the requirements of a given prescription without thinking consciously about it. I believe Hart (1961, pp. 23–24 and 49–64) has something like this in mind when he refers to the "habit of obedience" with respect to laws. And I am convinced that habits constitute a widespread phenomenon in connection with many problems of compliance. Therefore, it is worth noting that the operation of habits is not incompatible with the occurrence of choice (though it does raise questions about the prospects for rational choice).

It seems clear that habits and practices are acquired through such processes as socialization, psychological conditioning, and constant repetition in the absence of conscious deliberation. This suggests the possibility of considerable cross-cultural variation. Thus, child rearing practices in some cultures stress compliance heavily while others condone or even encourage various forms of permissiveness. Similarly, institutions such as schools and other large organizations place more stress on the inculcation of habits of compliance in some social systems than in others (Bronfenbrenner, 1970). Though this is a topic that clearly requires more study, it may well make sense to think of some cultures as compliance cultures.

There is no reason to expect habits and practices to be equally influential with respect to all problems of compliance. Other things being equal, habits and practices are likely to emerge as simplifying devices in coping with compliance problems that exhibit the following characteristics: (1) marginal importance or low intensity, (2) frequent recurrence, and (3) little tendency to change over time. Under such conditions, habits may prove quite helpful to subjects facing numerous choices at the same time, and actors may be consciously aware of the existence of such habits without experiencing any incentives to eradicate them.

This suggests several additional comments about the links between rationality and habits or practices. It is clear that it will sometimes be rational for public authorities to attempt to inculcate habits in groups of subjects through such processes as socialization. Though this will involve a significant initial investment, it is likely to be a particularly effective means of achieving high levels of compliance in situations involving highly repetitive behavior. Moreover, there is no reason to conclude that the development of habits or practices is irrational from the point of view of subjects. A choice made out of habit can hardly be regarded as rational per se, but actors can deliberately decide to cope with certain compliance problems on the basis of habit. This follows from the behavioral assumptions set forth earlier that numerous choice problems occur simultaneously and that subjects have limited decision-making capacity.

In concluding this section on bases of compliance, I offer the following general observations. While it is analytically useful to differentiate various incentives in the realm of compliance, there is every reason to believe that two or more of these incentives will operate simultaneously in most real-world situations. Accordingly, subjects will frequently experience problems of aggregation in making choices. This will serve to increase the attractiveness of simplifying devices like the development of general policies to cover groups of similar compliance problems.[20]

Next, this analysis demonstrates the inappropriateness of placing primary emphasis on enforcement as is often done in discussions of compliance. Enforcement is no doubt a sufficient condition for the achievement of compliance in many situations, but I can see no reason to regard it as a necessary condition in most realms of human activity. Finally, it seems evident that the various types of incentives I have identified are not equally easy to manipulate by public authorities. Rewards and punishments are subject to more immediate manipulation than social pressures or feelings of obligation. Similarly, it may take a generation or more for a public authority to inculcate effective habits of compliance through processes of socialization, whereas punishments can be introduced or altered almost immediately. This is no doubt one source of the widespread tendency to focus on enforcement (or inducement) in discussions of compliance policies. Nevertheless, it is far from clear that this orientation is rational. In the long run, at least, it will sometimes be more efficient to pursue compliance through methods of altering incentive systems other than those associated with the use of rewards or punishments.

THE ROLE OF RELEVANT OTHERS

So far, I have been examining the bases of compliance as though our actor were the only one making compliance choices. To be sure, other

[20] Alternatively, subjects may develop some lexicographic ordering with respect to bases of compliance. That is, they may rank the various bases in terms of precedence.

actors appeared on the scene in discussions of social pressures, reciprocity, and the like, but it was never explicitly suggested that these others were facing parallel compliance choices. This perspective conveys a distorted picture of most real-world situations. In most cases, subject groups contain sets of actors who must make choices with respect to compliance at roughly the same time, and the individual actor is generally aware of this fact. In this section, then, I want to consider the compliance choices of the individual who knows that others will be making similar choices more or less simultaneously.

Consider first a situation in which a group of actors have developed rules designed to avoid underinvestment in the supply of collective goods or overinvestment in the exploitation of common property resources.[21] Suppose that these rules specify when actors are expected to make contributions or to refrain from exploitation but that there are no compliance mechanisms capable of employing punishments or rewards associated with them. Is it rational for the self-interested individual to comply with these rules? The answer is that it depends on the estimates the individual makes of the probable behavior of the other members of the group.[22] If the individual estimates that most of the others will violate the rules, it will do him no good to comply since the collective goods will not be supplied and the common property resources will be overexploited in any case. Conversely, if the individual believes that almost all the others in the group will comply with the rules, he may be able to violate with impunity becoming a free rider with respect to the collective goods and enjoying asymmetrical advantages with respect to the exploitation of the resources. However, there is a range of intermediate cases in which the rational individual may find it worthwhile to comply with the rules. These are cases in which the level of compliance on the part of others is such that compliance on the part of our individual will make a discernible difference in the probability of achieving the relevant group goals. The range of levels of compliance on the part of others over which this condition holds will vary from case to case. Nevertheless, the individual actor will need to make some estimate of the probable behavior of other members of the group in making his own decisions about compliance in these situations.

Now consider a case in which compliance stems from feelings of obligation, the relevant obligation being formulated in symmetrical terms (Pennock and Chapman, 1970). Suppose, for example, that I feel an obligation to keep my promises, but only to the extent that others in my group do so as well. Similarly, suppose that I feel an obligation to refrain from cheating on my income tax returns so long as I have reason to believe that others are not doing so, but that I would feel justified in cheating if it

---

[21] For a clear case study of these problems see Eckert (1975).
[22] For a more formal treatment of this calculation see Frohlich and Oppenheimer (1970).

became clear to me that many of my fellow group members were doing so as well. In cases of this type, the individual will find it of crucial importance to formulate estimates of the probable behavior of others in deciding whether he himself should comply or violate. Note also that while compliance may remain high so long as the members of the group trust each other to comply, violations by a relatively small number of members can precipitate a rapid breakdown of compliance throughout the group as a whole. I believe phenomena of this type are common in many real-world situations.

Several illustrations of an entirely different nature will serve to demonstrate the pervasiveness of interdependencies in decision making about compliance. Let us assume that you are attempting to calculate the probability of being detected, or punished, or both, in the event that you choose to violate a given behavioral prescription. Assume also that there is a public authority possessing a compliance mechanism of a certain finite size and capacity. What is the probability that your violation will be detected or punished?[23] Up to a point, the compliance mechanism will be able to handle all violations simultaneously so that the probability of being detected or punished will not be affected by the behavior of others. Beyond this point, however, the relevant probability will be a function of how many other members of the group choose to violate the prescription in question during the same time period. That is, the chances that your violation will be detected or punished will go down (often quite rapidly) as the number of other members of the group engaging in violations goes up. In the realm of criminal behavior, for example, there are many situations in which the capacity of compliance mechanisms relative to the number of violations is such that the probability of being caught and punished is extremely low (Robinson, 1977). Under these circumstances, any subject attempting to compute the expected value of violating a particular behavioral prescription will have a lively interest in estimating how many other members of the group will engage in violations during the same time period.

It is possible to carry this line of argument a step further and to consider the possibility of effective coordination among violators. Thus, an actor contemplating a violation will be interested in estimating the probability that he can join a group of violators capable of taking steps to reduce the expected costs to him of his violation. An example that comes readily to mind involves gangs or crime rings, which are often capable of protecting their members by deterring or buying off enforcement officers. But this is not the only context in which coordination among violators is relevant. For example, groups of protesters engaging in deliberate acts of civil disobedience may band together to raise defense funds and to employ

[23] This issue is treated relatively formally in Frohlich and Oppenheimer (1971: esp. Ch. 8). See also the discussion in Frohlich and Oppenheimer (1974).

superior legal talent in behalf of their individual members. And there are sometimes advantages to be gained from the mere presence of numbers. Thus, if all the motorists on a given highway tacitly collude in breaking the speed limit, it will be virtually impossible for enforcement officers to do much about it.[24] In all these cases, then, any individual contemplating violation will be interested in estimating not only how many others will violate during the same time period but also the chances of his being able to join a coordinated group of violators capable of giving him some protection. There is no doubt that this factor will have a substantial impact on the expected value of violation in many real-world situations.

These illustrations demonstrate that subjects will typically have a well-developed interest in contemplating the probable behavior of relevant others as they go about making their own choices in the realm of compliance. In addition, they exhibit a common element that raises important problems from an analytic point of view. Specifically, strategic interaction is apt to play a prominent role in all these situations (Young, 1975, Introduction). That is, the subject attempting to estimate the probable behavior of relevant others will be aware that these others will simultaneously be trying to assess his own probable behavior and that this can easily initiate a logical regress. In large groups, individuals will often cope with the problem of strategic interaction by making blanket assumptions about the behavior of the relevant others and proceeding with their own cost-benefit calculations on this basis. But there is no reason to assume that all actors will employ the same blanket assumptions, and the standard of rationality is not sufficient to single out any particular assumption of this type as preferred in normative terms. In smaller groups, on the other hand, individual actors often engage in explicit interactions with relevant others so that the problem of strategic interaction can be dealt with through bargaining or negotiation (Young, 1975). Individuals in such groups may even deliberately coordinate their actions in order to make it easier to include estimates of the behavior of relevant others in decisions pertaining to compliance. But in either case, students of compliance will have to reckon with the phenomenon of strategic interaction in their efforts to understand the choices of individual subjects with respect to compliance and violation.

[24] This will be especially true wherever courts are committed to the principle of equal protection under the law.

CHAPTER 3

Compliance in the international system

As I indicated in chapter 1, I propose to explore in depth the problem of compliance as it arises in the international system. To this end I shall treat the international system as a member of the class of highly decentralized social systems. Decentralized systems are those in which both authority and power are distributed horizontally rather than hierarchically. Large social systems of this type are often described as stateless societies, but decentralized social systems occur at many other levels as well. The concept of decentralization identifies a spectrum of possibilities rather than a dichotomy. There are extensive variations in the ways social systems distribute authority and power, and it is not helpful to attempt arbitrarily to group all systems under the headings of centralized and decentralized. In this discussion, however, I shall be concerned with common features of social systems that lie well along toward the decentralized end of the spectrum. While it is possible to regard highly decentralized social systems as anarchies in the formal or technical sense of the term, such systems will not inevitably be characterized by disorder or chaos (Shatz, 1971, pp. xi–xxix). Nevertheless, highly decentralized social systems lack rulers or centralized institutions of government, and this is the defining characteristic of anarchy in the technical sense.

It does not, I think, require much argument to establish that the international system is a member of the class of highly decentralized social systems. Consider first the issue of authority. So long as the doctrine of state sovereignty remained unchallenged, the international system was actually an extreme type of decentralized society. This situation has been modified somewhat by the introduction of universal international organizations like the United Nations. But these developments were never intended to produce a qualitative shift in the distribution of authority within the system. And, in practice, the operation of organizations like the United Nations has led only to the most modest movement of the international system toward centralized authority (Kaplan and Katzenbach, 1961, especially chap. 11). Power also is distributed in a distinctly decentralized fashion in the international system. I do not mean to suggest that power is distributed evenly among the members, and the changing fortunes of individual members generate continuous shifts in its distribution.[1] But no single member (or cohesive group of members) dominates the system in terms of effective power. Moreover, the international system lacks institutions possessing anything remotely approaching a monopoly over the use of legitimate force within the system. I shall not attempt to calibrate the spectrum between centralization and decentralization in order to determine the precise locus of the international system in it. It is sufficient for my purposes in this essay simply to establish that the international system belongs to the set of highly decentralized social systems.

COMPLIANCE IN DECENTRALIZED SOCIAL SYSTEMS

In this section, I want to consider a number of attributes common to all decentralized social systems with respect to compliance. Any conclusions arising from this discussion will be fully applicable to the case of the international system.

Extreme cases

It is widely assumed that the achievement of compliance in highly decentralized social systems is extremely difficult. Those who make this assumption generally regard some form of hierarchical organization as a necessary condition for compliance, and anarchy as a recipe for extreme disorder.[2] What is the basis of this point of view? I believe it rests on a tendency to single out certain extreme cases and to equate all problems of compliance in decentralized social systems with these extreme cases. To see this, let us consider a concrete example. Imagine a large group of individuals packed together in a crowded subway car. Assume also that there is no official present to detect violations of behavioral prescriptions and to apprehend violators. What are the chances that these individuals will comply with pertinent prescriptions concerning appropriate behavior while entering the car, riding in the car, and exiting from the car?

This situation exhibits a number of characteristics that combine to make the achievement of compliance difficult. First, the members of the

---

[1] On the problems of analyzing the distribution of power in empirical terms, see Hart (1976).

[2] To illustrate, compare the views of Hobbes (1962) on this question with those of leading anarchist thinkers like Kropotkin. For an account of anarchist thinking on such questions see Guerin (1970).

group typically do not know each other and have no previous experiences with each other. Consequently, they will not possess stable expectations and viable rules at the outset. Second, interactions of this type are fleeting, and noniterative, so that the discipline of time cannot be expected to work effectively. Third, the membership of the group will fluctuate constantly as individuals enter the car and exit from the car. This makes it difficult for stable expectations to arise out of the situation itself. Fourth, mechanisms for the coordination of expectations are typically weak. It is extremely difficult for any single individual to exhibit effective leadership, and there are no built-in institutional arrangements to facilitate coordination. Fifth, the group will be sufficiently large so that it will be hard to develop effective rules through explicit processes of bargaining and negotiation. The shifting membership of the group will also act as a barrier to the emergence of such processes. Sixth, the members of the group are likely to have highly negative expectations about the behavior of the others because most of them will have had negative experiences in previous situations of a similar kind. Under the circumstances, members of the group are not likely to be willing to take significant chances in the hopes of encouraging compliant behavior on the part of others.

Given all these difficulties, is there anything that can be done to strengthen the incentives of individuals to comply with behavioral prescriptions in situations of this sort? About the only possibility I can see lies in the realm of long-term socialization (Bronfenbrenner, 1970). That is, it may be possible to encourage the development of a generalized compliance culture that serves to structure the behavior of individuals in a variety of day-to-day situations. In *a priori* terms, this prospect seems unlikely: what reason does the individual subway rider have to rely on the socialization of a group of unknown others to ensure that they will comply with the pertinent behavioral prescriptions? Empirically, however, one can observe that compliance cultures are by no means inoperative in such situations. While there is clearly a great deal of variation from one situation to another, there are societies in which a high proportion of the members have internalized strong social norms concerning compliance with a variety of behavioral prescriptions. Subway riding is a much more orderly process in some societies than in others even in the absence of enforcement officers.[3] In my judgment, it would be well worth investigating this range of phenomena on a cross-cultural basis.

Compliance without organization

It is relevant to inquire whether extreme cases of the type considered above constitute the exception or the rule. I see no reason to conclude that the extreme cases are predominant in most social systems. There are

[3] Note, however, that even in Great Britain, where behavior in public places is notably orderly, riding on the underground during rush hour is an arduous experience.

numerous situations in which subjects left to their own calculations in the absence of any organized sanctions nevertheless exhibit high levels of compliance. In Switzerland, for example, many public telephones and buses are operated on what amounts to an honor system in which compliance with prescriptions concerning payment is essentially voluntary. And it would not be difficult to compile a long list of other examples in which compliance typically occurs in the absence of any organized compliance mechanisms. How do we account for behavior of this type?

Above all, it seems clear that there are numerous situations in which simple self-interest dictates compliance. That is, when looked at in simple cost-benefit terms, the expected benefits of compliance often outweigh the costs without regard to any prospects of enforcement, inducement, or social pressure. In some cases, this flows from the fact that noncompliance carries its own penalty. This is true, for example, of rules requiring employees to undergo annual physical examinations or students to take introductory courses in a given subject before enrolling in advanced courses. In many other cases, the prospects of counter violations, retaliation, undermining the general viability of the prescriptions in question, or reducing the opportunities for profitable interactions in the future are sufficient to make the expected costs of violations outweigh the possible gains. There can be no doubt that compliant behavior often stems directly from calculations of this type and that it would be a mistake to exaggerate the role of organized compliance mechanisms in eliciting such behavior even in relatively centralized social systems. This is especially true whenever the members of the system in question think in relatively long-run terms[4] and whenever they consider the broader implications of their behavior as well as the immediate consequences of choices.

There is, however, one major class of situations in which simple self-interest calculations are not sufficient to induce compliance. These are situations in which individuals experience free-rider incentives with respect to the relevant prescriptions. That is, they approve of the existence of the prescriptions and they want others to comply with them. But their preferred outcome would be compliance on the part of everyone else coupled with noncompliance for themselves. This would permit them to enjoy an orderly social system while reaping the benefits of noncompliance at the same time.[5] But note the logical implication of such calculations. If a large proportion of the members of the social system think this way, compliance will be uncommon and the social system will degenerate toward a disorderly (or even Hobbesian) state of nature. Accordingly, the individual

[4] In more technical terms, this condition can be said to hold when decision makers do not discount future benefits heavily in computing the present value of alternatives. For a clear discussion of discounting see Zeckhauser and Shaefer (1968, pp. 87–91).

[5] The issue here is analogous to the collective goods problem. See Olson (1965) and Frohlich, Oppenheimer, and Young (1971).

will obtain neither the advantages of an orderly social system nor the benefits of violation coupled with compliance on the part of others.[6]

The classic response to this problem is the introduction of some arrangement whereby all members of the group agree to allow themselves to be coerced into complying with behavioral prescriptions. But this requires the development of some enforcement mechanism, which is clearly incompatible with the continued existence of a highly decentralized social system. In fact, efforts to resolve problems of this type constitute a standard justification for introducing government and increasing the level of centralization in social systems (Locke, 1966). I have some doubt, however, whether the introduction of some such enforcement mechanism constitutes a necessary condition for the achievement of compliance under these conditions.[7] Individuals operating in highly decentralized social systems will know that they cannot rely upon a government or some other centralized public authority to maintain order and to preserve the social fabric of the system. Therefore, they are likely to be far more concerned with the social consequences of their behavior than they would be in a centralized system, where such concerns can be allowed to atrophy without causing undue harm, at least in the short run (Taylor, 1976, especially pp. 134–140). Accordingly, an individual experiencing free-rider incentives may well think twice about the broader implications of giving in to these incentives in a decentralized system whereas he might attempt to become a free rider in a more centralized system. Thus, the factors in the calculus of the individual regarding compliance will not necessarily be identical in decentralized and centralized systems.

In addition, there is no reason to assume that feelings of obligation will be inoperative as a basis of compliance in highly decentralized social systems, although such feelings may be linked more closely to explicit consent in such systems (Hart, 1958 and Fuller, 1958). Subjects are apt to regard themselves as highly autonomous in decentralized systems and to object to prescriptions that they themselves have not agreed to explicitly. But none of this suggests the irrelevance of obligation as a basis of their compliance. On the contrary, obligations may sometimes become even more binding in decentralized social systems than in centralized ones because there is no authoritative agency capable of exempting a subject from the force of an obligation under special or extenuating circumstances. Finally, there is no reason to conclude that the development of an effective compliance culture is necessarily infeasible in a highly decentralized social system, even though it is true that such a social system will lack a government or some other centralized public authority capable of fostering the

---

[6] A more rigorous analysis of this problem could be constructed using the prisoner's dilemma paradigm, developed in Rapoport and Chammah (1965).

[7] Note also that one might question whether the introduction of such an enforcement mechanism constitutes a *sufficient* condition.

emergence of a compliance culture on a systematic basis. In fact, widespread social norms concerning compliance may well emerge under such conditions precisely because of the absence of a centralized public authority (Mair, 1962 and Hoebel, 1954).

Decentralized institutions

Although decentralized social systems do not have centralized and formally organized governments, it would be a mistake to assume that they entirely lack institutions relating to compliance. A little reflection will make it clear that various institutional arrangements are perfectly compatible with the general condition of decentralization in social systems (Burke, Legatski, and Woodhead, 1975).

It is possible to distinguish at least three characteristics of compliance mechanisms in decentralized systems. First, activities relating to compliance are often performed by a wide range of actors rather than by a single actor specialized to the task of handling compliance problems. For example, some systems have authorized self-help arrangements in which it is entirely acceptable for individual actors to mete out sanctions under specified circumstances. Second, there are many systems in which compliance mechanisms are developed for individual functional areas, with the result that there is no centralized agency concerned with problems of compliance in general. In the international system, there are distinct arrangements for maritime transport, air transport, commodity trade, monetary transactions, specialized problems relating to the management of natural resources, and so forth (Tauber, 1969 and Fisher, 1971). Third, it is common in decentralized social systems for separate institutions to handle different aspects of the overall problem of compliance. Thus, there may be quite distinct arrangements for inspection and information gathering, the application of prescriptions, and the organization of sanctions (Oliver, 1971).

It is not uncommon for systems to develop institutionalized arrangements for inspection and surveillance even in the absence of clear-cut procedures relating to the other aspects of compliance (Falk and Barnet, 1965). The extent to which such arrangements become important will of course be a function of the chances for subjects to engage in clandestine violations. In some areas, it is exceedingly difficult to prevent violations from coming to the attention of others, and explicit arrangements for inspection are relatively unimportant. In other cases, however, the knowledge that there is a high probability that violations will be detected may be a substantial incentive for individuals to comply, even if they do not expect sanctions to follow detection.[8] This is so because of the possible

---

[8] I am reminded in this context of the traditional Harvard aphorism that it is acceptable for a gentleman to do as he pleases so long as he is not caught doing it.

behavior of others toward a known violator. For example, an individual who is known to violate the injunction that promises should be kept will experience considerable difficulty in reaching agreements with others in a wide range of situations.

In some decentralized systems, there are *ad hoc* tribunals which are authorized to judge whether specified behavioral prescriptions have been violated in disputed cases (Tauber, 1969). In other decentralized systems, such decisions are left to the individual members of the system. The point I want to emphasize here, however, is that there is an important difference between leaving such decisions to the individual members on a *de facto* basis on the one hand and explicitly authorizing individual members to render such judgments in terms of well-defined criteria on the other. In the latter case, individual members are officially deputized by the community to render judgments on its behalf concerning violations of behavioral prescriptions occurring within their own jurisdictions (Bilder, 1974). Such arrangements are not uncommon in systems where jurisdictions are clearly demarcated either in territorial or in functional terms, and they deserve to be considered carefully as a response to the problem of developing compliance mechanisms in highly decentralized social systems.

The organization of sanctions against those who violate behavioral prescriptions is typically left in the hands of the individual members in highly decentralized social systems (Reisman, 1971 and Doxey, 1971). There is a critical distinction between cases in which the use of such sanctions is authorized by the community and cases in which actors simply proceed on their own to coerce others. Situations of the former type are well-known as self-help procedures and deserve recognition as an important type of institutionalized arrangement for highly decentralized social systems. In many primitive systems, for example, it is perfectly acceptable for an injured party (or a member of his family) to take matters into his own hands, punishing an offender in accordance with the customs of the community. Situations of the latter type, however, do not really belong to the category of compliance mechanisms at all.

There are some decentralized social systems, moreover, in which efforts are made to develop procedures to coordinate sanctions, even though the actual application of sanctions is left in the hands of the individual members. Such agencies typically make recommendations concerning whether or not sanctions should be employed, and they ordinarily attempt to orchestrate the sanctions employed by individual members in order to maximize their impact on violators. Nevertheless, individual members are not bound to follow the proposals of the agency (Doxey, 1971).

It is evident from this discussion that highly decentralized social systems may possess an extensive array of compliance mechanisms, even though they have no centralized public authorities. There are, however, certain standard and relatively serious problems that afflict the operation of compliance mechanisms in such systems. Perhaps most fundamental is the fact that the individual members of these systems often experience free-rider incentives. If high levels of compliance occur, the benefits will accrue to all members of the system whether or not they contribute to the achievement of this result. Therefore, the usual problems associated with the supply of collective goods will arise, and there will be a distinct tendency toward underinvestment in compliance mechanisms. A little reflection suggests that this problem is of great importance in real-world cases. It is indeed difficult to elicit substantial contributions for compliance mechanisms from, say, the individual members of the United Nations (Stoessinger and Associates, 1964). Such problems constitute a standard justification for proposals to introduce more centralized public authorities in decentralized social systems. But it is by no means clear that the crucial problem here lies in the absence of centralized institutions. There is little reason to conclude that the *pro forma* creation of formal institutions in the absence of deeper changes would lead to markedly different results.

The pursuit of compliance in decentralized social systems will often be afflicted by disagreements about the scope, the domain, and the required actions of the relevant behavioral prescriptions. I do not believe that the pertinent behavioral prescriptions will be unusually hard to formulate or to articulate, but decentralization does make it difficult to obtain authoritative interpretations when disagreements arise among individual members. And, unless there is an unusually high degree of consensus in the system, regular resort to self-interpretation is likely to increase continuously the level of uncertainty and ambiguity surrounding many behavioral prescriptions (McDougal, Lasswell, and Miller, 1967). The importance of this problem will obviously vary with the circumstances of the individual social system. It will undoubtedly be most severe in decentralized social systems characterized by low levels of social consensus and by the prevalence of highly complex behavioral prescriptions. As a generalization, however, it seems accurate to conclude that highly decentralized systems will ordinarily possess a smaller set of clearly formulated and widely acknowledged behavioral prescriptions than highly centralized social systems.

The use of decentralized compliance mechanisms is also likely to lead to problems in determining when violations have actually occurred. Those accused of violations by other members of the social system will often refuse to acknowledge the validity of the accusation, claiming that their actions have been misrepresented or misconstrued in some way. And the absence of any centralized agency capable of making authoritative decisions in such cases will make it difficult to resolve disputes decisively. Except in particularly simple or unusually clear-cut cases, therefore, it will often be hard to determine if and when serious violations have occurred in highly decentralized social systems.

Decentralization and externalities

The negative externalities or by-products associated with compliance mechanisms flow mostly from the activities of centralized public authorities like formal governments. In general, they involve such things as invasions of privacy, pressures toward regimentation and conformity, the proliferation of bureaucratic red tape, the loss of spontaneity, and the suppression of incentives to innovate. All these phenomena will be less prominent in highly decentralized social systems.

I do not mean to imply by this, however, that the decentralized compliance mechanisms discussed earlier in this chapter will generate no externalities in their own right. It seems clear that compliance mechanisms of this type will produce certain unintended side effects of their own. As I have already argued, compliance is possible to achieve in highly decentralized social systems, but it may well be that the overall level of compliance is lower in these systems than in those that are more highly centralized. To the extent that this is the case, it seems likely that an atmosphere of uncertainty and even fear will be an unintended by-product of the operation of highly decentralized compliance mechanisms. This is so because the members of such systems will not be able to rely on the high levels of predictability and order associated with systems in which compliance can ordinarily be taken for granted (Emmet, 1972). In addition, when prescriptions are applied and sanctions organized by a wide range of individual actors on an autonomous basis, it is reasonable to assume that unprincipled and capricious behavior will occur from time to time. In such systems, there is no centralized agency that can be expected to handle similar problems of compliance in a like fashion under most circumstances.

Until recently, it has been customary to criticize decentralization and to acclaim centralization as the wave of the future in most social systems. Though the relevant arguments are by no means confined to the realm of compliance, they are just as applicable to that problem as to other issues. At present, we are witnessing a shift toward the condemnation of centralization coupled with a rather uncritical perspective on the alleged benefits of decentralization (Levy, 1972). My analysis of compliance, however, strongly indicates the importance of adopting a critical stance toward both of these orientations. With respect to the problem of compliance at least, both centralization and decentralization have costs as well as benefits. Moreover, it seems clear that compliance mechanisms should be carefully tailored to the particular attributes of the social system in question. For example in the extreme cases I described earlier in this chapter, the argument for centralized compliance mechanisms is apt to be compelling. But in other cases, it may be feasible to rely on highly decentralized arrangements, thereby avoiding some of the standard externalities associated with more centralized compliance mechanisms.

DISTINCTIVE FEATURES OF THE INTERNATIONAL SYSTEM

As I indicated at the beginning of this chapter, the international system is a member of the class of highly decentralized social systems. But it also exhibits a number of distinctive features that have important implications for the achievement of compliance. The purpose of this section is to identify the most critical of these features and to assess their consequences.

Nature of the subjects

There is some disagreement concerning the identity of the members of the international system (Young, 1972). Earlier thinking regarding this issue typically restricted membership in the system to the category of sovereign states. But this perspective has come under increasing attack in recent years. No one wishes to deny that states continue to constitute an important class of members of the international system. However, there is a growing feeling that other entities, such as international organizations, multinational corporations, and transnational interest groups, should be regarded as autonomous actors in the system as well (Keohane and Nye, 1977).

No matter where we draw the line regarding membership in the international system, several points about international actors are worth noting with reference to the problem of compliance. First, the number of actors in the system is relatively small, no more than a few hundred by most criteria of membership in use at this time. While the system does not belong to the category of small groups as that concept is generally employed in social psychology, the number of actors involved is small compared with the massive numbers of autonomous actors we are used to thinking of in discussions of domestic societies. Above all, this means that it is possible to focus on the behavior of well-defined subjects rather than conceptualizing the problem of compliance largely in actuarial terms. Moreover, it suggests that the actors will typically consider the behavior of specific others rather than some undifferentiated environment in making computations regarding the costs and benefits of compliance. That is, they will make explicit calculations concerning the expected reactions of other individual members of the system in making choices between compliance and violation.[9] Because of this, the international equivalent of social pressure can be expected to be an important basis of compliance in this system, even in the absence of organized agencies dealing with enforcement and inducement (Kiesler and Kiesler, 1969).

Equally important is the fact that the actors in the international system are collective or corporate entities. Following the orientation of most theories of choice, I have been proceeding so far in my analysis of compliance on the assumption that the subjects of behavioral prescriptions are

[9] For an extended discussion of this phenomenon in connection with the concept of strategic interaction see Young (1975).

more or less integrated individuals (or at least that it is reasonable to think of them in this way). Thus, I have generally predicated my analysis on the premises that subjects are capable of formulating clear-cut preference orderings over sets of alternatives and that their behavior does not involve the coordination of a number of autonomous or semiautonomous component units. But such premises are clearly inappropriate when it comes to an examination of the external behavior of the members of the international system. In this case, external behavior is clearly a product of relatively complex internal processes (Allison, 1971 and Steinbruner, 1974). Accordingly, the standard models of individual choice are apt to prove no more than suggestive. Alternative models are needed, designed explicitly to take into account the internal make-up of the collective or corporate entities characteristic of the international system.

It is possible to examine the external behavior of the actors in the international system from a number of points of view. No one of the resultant models is objectively correct; each highlights different factors. There are three approaches which strike me as particularly useful. First, the compliance choices of these actors can be conceptualized as outcomes of internal processes of bargaining and negotiation (Young, 1975 and Zartman, 1976). Each collective entity is thus viewed as a set of interdependent actors with divergent but not strictly competitive interests. Each of these actors attempts to maximize its own gains, but it must do so by bargaining with the others because of the postulated condition of interdependence. Accordingly, the external behavior of the collective entity flows from the bargains struck in its internal processes. The basic implication of this perspective for the problem of compliance is that collective entities are not likely to follow a consistent or undeviating path with respect to their external behavior. Unless one internal actor achieves an overwhelmingly dominant position, the entity is apt to shift back and forth between compliance and violation in response to the dynamics of its internal bargaining processes (Neustadt, 1970).

A second perspective on the external behavior of collective entities focuses on bureaucratic behavior and the operation of organizational routines (March and Simon, 1958). Large and complex collective entities invariably develop elaborate organizational arrangements and procedures that govern their external behavior. To understand that behavior, therefore, it is necessary to examine carefully these internal structures together with the behavior of the bureaucrats who operate within them. In addition, it is commonly argued that rules constitute an essential feature of bureaucracies and that routinized compliance with rules is a deeply engrained norm among bureaucrats.[10] Consequently, this perspective suggests relatively optimistic conclusions concerning the prospects of achieving

[10] The classic formulation of this point is that of Max Weber. See Gerth and Mills (1958, pp. 196–244). For a recent formulation of similar arguments see Fisher (1969).

high levels of compliance in the international system. Once a behavioral prescription becomes a standard operating procedure or norm of the bureaucracy, the tendency to follow rules on a routinized basis will take over as a determinant of external behavior (Chayes, 1972).

A third approach to the external behavior of collective entities is to view them as small groups or teams. Here the idea is to identify a small number of individual actors who constitute the crucial decision makers within the entity and to focus on the interactions among these actors. The external behavior of the entity then becomes a product of group dynamics, and it is possible to apply various insights from social psychology and the theory of teams to this problem (Thibaut and Kelley, 1959 and Buchanan, 1965). In general, the implications of this perspective seem considerably less optimistic than those of the bureaucratic perspective with respect to the prospects of achieving compliance at the international level. Of course, it is dangerous to overgeneralize in this realm. Nevertheless, there is some evidence to suggest that groups are apt to engage in riskier behavior and to exhibit greater aggressiveness than individuals. This is because individuals operating in groups sometimes push each other toward more extreme positions, and they may lack a sense of personal responsibility for the behavior of the group as such (Janis, 1972).

Regardless of how we choose to think about the external behavior of collective entities, it is possible to make a number of general statements about the relevance of various bases of compliance to them. To begin with, there are some bases of compliance that simply do not apply to collective entities. Thus, a collective entity is not capable of experiencing feelings of obligation in its own right. Individuals occupying official positions within such an entity may well feel obligations, but the entity itself has no capacity to experience such feelings. Moreover, officials change rapidly, and it is quite common for new officials not to feel a strong sense of obligation to comply with commitments made by their predecessors. This is the source of the well-known rule that collective entities have short "memories" when it comes to commitments and problems of compliance. Similarly, collective entities cannot be socialized, so that it does not make sense to think of them in terms of the development of a compliance culture. Again, individuals within collectivities (for example, various bureaucrats) are subject to socialization, and they may well exert considerable influence on the external behavior of these entities. But this is hardly equivalent to socializing the subjects of the relevant behavioral prescriptions themselves. At best, it requires a two-step process with respect to which there is considerable room for slippage.

By the same token, there are some bases of compliance that do not affect individuals as such but that often play an important role in determining the external behavior of collective entities. I have already mentioned the case of organizational routines and bureaucratic behavior. This force for compliance works a little like a deeply engrained habit in an individual. But it is undoubtedly even more difficult to overcome because it typically involves large numbers of individuals whose behavior would have to be coordinated in order to achieve significant changes (Chayes, 1972). In addition, there are internal forces of a political nature that commonly operate to propel collective entities toward compliance with accepted behavioral prescriptions. Leaders become committed to the maintenance of rules they have helped to negotiate. Opposition groups can focus on any indications that violations are being encouraged as a way of attacking incumbent leaders. And vested interests are apt to grow up over time around the continued operation of existing behavioral prescriptions. In short, whereas an individual can simply weigh the costs and benefits of compliance and reach the conclusion that violation will pay in a given case, various forms of internal opposition will ordinarily have to be overcome before a collective entity can engage in noncompliant behavior.

Finally, a special feature of the compliance problem for collective entities, is the question of who is ultimately responsible for violations (Taylor, 1970a and Taylor, 1970b). If the entity itself is held responsible, individuals are not likely to feel the force of sanctions or social pressure strongly. Yet, it is ultimately the actions of individuals which determine the external behavior of collective entities. Alternatively, if individuals are made responsible for the behavior of collectivities, other problems arise. One approach is to designate the sovereign as the responsible agent. But how is it possible to sanction a sovereign, and what is to be done when sovereignty resides with a group rather than with an individual? To the best of my knowledge, there are no entirely satisfactory answers to these questions, at least at the international level. There can be little doubt that these ambiguities pose difficulties for the achievement of high levels of compliance in some situations. While it would be wrong to overemphasize this factor, the prospect of escaping the immediate consequences of violations will undoubtedly serve to make individuals within collective entities less cautious about noncompliant behavior in some situations.

Character of the prescriptions

The behavioral prescriptions that arise in the international system share numerous characteristics with similar prescriptions operative in other social systems. Nevertheless, there are several attributes of these prescriptions which are distinctive. International prescriptions commonly take the form of understandings, agreements, or treaties among specified sets of actors in contrast to more general or open-ended rules for the system as a whole. That is, the principal prescriptions of the international system are relatively closed agreements among well-defined groups of actors rather than broadly formulated rules applicable to any actor who finds himself in a given situation. In this sense, international prescriptions bear a distinct resemblance to contracts, in contrast to laws, in municipal systems. Morover, these agreements typically deal with the problem of compliance in an *ad hoc* fashion; the arrangements they encompass are limited strictly to the agreements in question. The prevalence of such agreements, therefore, does not encourage the emergence of more centralized institutions pertaining to compliance.

Related to this is the fact that explicit consent is of central importance to the operation of behavioral prescriptions in the international system. Thus, the actors generally reject ideas of obligation emanating from mere membership in the system or various forms of tacit consent (Pitkin, 1965 and Pitkin, 1966). In many other social systems, when an individual actor becomes a member, he is assumed to accept the prevailing set of behavioral prescriptions in the system unless he makes a specific point of rejecting one or more of them. In the international system, however, new members can and often do reject existing prescriptions, and there is no automatic presumption that they have accepted them simply by accepting membership in the system.[11] The critical role of explicit consent is of course obvious with respect to agreements and treaties. However, the role of explicit consent is unusually important in this system even in the case of other types of prescriptions. For example, there has been some debate about the extent to which such things as United Nations resolutions can be regarded as binding on all members of the international system.[12] I do not mean to dismiss these devices as insignificant, but it seems to me that it would be a serious mistake to ignore the differences between the international system and most domestic social systems with respect to this question of explicit consent. Among other things, this implies that the set of widely accepted behavioral prescriptions will be smaller in the international system than it is in other social systems in which ideas of tacit consent are more viable.

Next, the behavioral prescriptions of the international system are more afflicted by ambiguity than those of many other social systems. In my judgment, the crucial source of this ambiguity does not lie in the often lamented fact that the international system lacks the centralized institutions of government we commonly associate with political communities (Mendlovitz, 1975). I would argue that this feature of the set of international prescriptions stems from two sources that are more fundamental than that. First, the system is both heterogeneous, in the sense that the interests of the actors diverge widely, and volatile, in the sense that patterns of relationships among the actors change rapidly. For these reasons, the status

[11] This is so, in practice, despite the provision of Article 4 of the United Nations Charter which specifies that a willingness to ". . . accept the obligations contained in the present Charter" is a condition for membership in the Organization.

[12] For an expansive view of the significance of United Nations resolutions see Falk (1966).

of individual prescriptions is responsive to changing relationships within the system itself, and it is often difficult to determine at any given time how specific prescriptions are regarded by various members of the system. Second, many important international prescriptions are intrinsically difficult to put into operation in real-world situations. It is simple enough to ban all nuclear tests in the atmosphere. But consider such prescriptions as the rules against aggression, the rules pertaining to nonintervention in the internal affairs of other actors, the rules concerning the recognition of new governments, the rules relating to the status of nonbelligerency, and the rules governing the conduct of overt hostilities (Kaplan and Katzenbach, 1961, especially part II). In all these cases, the nature of the behavior in question makes it difficult to eliminate substantial elements of ambiguity surrounding the relevant prescriptions.

In many social systems, violations of behavioral prescriptions remain largely private affairs; they do not become matters of widespread public attention. In some cases, such violations simply go undetected. In others, they are not of interest to many members of the system even if they are detected. In the international system, however, the violation of behavioral prescriptions is typically a much more public affair. Partly, this stems from the fact that the system is a relatively small one in which each actor is generally well aware of what the others are doing.[13] It is also attributable to the fact that many international violations automatically become matters of public record. This is true, for example, of most violations of the rules against aggression or the rules pertaining to the status of nonbelligerency. But there are many cases at the international level in which the violating actor himself must sooner or later reveal his noncompliant behavior in order to reap the benefits associated with the violation. Thus, it is typically impossible to reap strategic advantages from violating an arms control agreement unless the violations are ultimately revealed in some dramatic fashion.[14] And the actor who violates an agreement to refrain from producing specified goods for an international market cannot benefit from his noncompliant behavior unless he reveals his violations openly.

Finally, I want to say something about the consequences of violating international prescriptions. The violation of any behavioral prescription is apt to be taken seriously by the actors immediately involved. But, the distinctive feature of international violations is that they are far more likely to have extensive collateral or systemic consequences than violations in

---

[13] The same phenomenon occurs in small communities composed of individual human beings. For a striking case study see Wylie (1974).

[14] Note, however, that this is not always the case. Secret testing to maintain technological capabilities may help to set the minds of policymakers at rest even if it is never revealed. Similarly, cheating on the permissible number of strategic delivery vehicles might have the psychological effect of increasing confidence in the effectiveness of deterrence even (or perhaps especially) if the cheating is never detected. I owe this point to the comments of Robert L. Butterworth.

other social systems. For example, the consequences of a murder in a typical domestic society seldom extend beyond the families and friends of the individuals immediately involved, unless the victim is a figure of critical importance in the society. An act of aggression at the international level, however, may precipitate violent conflict involving many members of the system. And most members of the system are apt to feel the impact of such violations, at least indirectly. This feature of the international system can be expected to have important implications for the problem of compliance. Briefly, all those actors who are likely to experience collateral damage from the noncompliant behavior of others can ordinarily be counted upon to exert considerable pressure for compliance in specific situations. While the international system lacks a centralized public authority, therefore, it does possess a well-informed "public," which can be counted on to express concern about the occurrence of violations and which can be expected to exert pressures for compliance on potential violators.

International institutions

It is undoubtedly true that the members of the international system are generally left to their own calculations in making choices concerning compliance. That is, behavior in this realm is not deeply affected by the activities of formal institutions organized at the systemic level. This is not to say that the subjects of international prescriptions will engage in noncompliant behavior lightly. It merely suggests that the activities of formal international institutions seldom play a crucial role in their decisions about compliance and violation. Nevertheless, it would be a mistake to conclude that international institutions are entirely irrelevant. The United Nations hardly conforms to our image of a centralized public authority. It was never intended to operate in this fashion, and its actual performance falls short of the relatively modest expectations incorporated in the Charter (Nicholas, 1962). Even so, actors in the international system cannot afford to ignore completely the actions of the Organization in making their own choices about compliance. Moreover, there is a considerable array of more specialized and decentralized institutions in the international system which have some relevance to the problem of compliance. The fact that these institutions are highly decentralized makes it easy to overlook their significance, but in fact they add up to a rather extensive network.

Inspection systems have been experimented with in a number of areas at the international level. For example, there are relatively well-developed inspection arrangements in some technical realms such as international air transport (Tauber, 1969), and substantial efforts have been made to introduce inspection systems relating to more highly politicized matters like the control of armaments (Falk and Barnet, 1965). Underlying many of these arrangements is the premise that inspection can play a significant role in eliciting compliance even in the absence of well-developed institutions for the organization of sanctions. Partly, this premise rests on the idea that other actors in the system are apt to react in such a way as to reduce the benefits of violations once they become aware of their occurrence. In some cases, however, it is also predicated on the idea of reducing the chances for an actor to gain major advantages through clandestine violations that can be revealed dramatically later on after extensive preparations have been made. It is worth noting here that considerable efforts have been made to develop international inspection procedures that are politically acceptable to the actors involved. Often this is essentially a matter of regulating certain externalities associated with international inspection. For example, attempts have been made in the realm of arms control to devise inspection systems capable of detecting violations of the relevant agreements without simultaneously obtaining too much information about the military preparations or other aspects of the societies in which the inspections are being carried out. Finally, it is important to note that international inspection is a function of the state of technology as well as the nature of the specific activities in question. Thus, there are cases in which technological advances have the effect of reducing the importance of international inspection systems by making it less and less feasible for actors to engage in otherwise undetected violations. Here too the area of arms control provides clear-cut examples.[15]

Traditionally, the application of international prescriptions was treated as a process that could not be subjected to institutionalization at the system level. The doctrine of state sovereignty led directly to the conclusion that each member of the system was to be its own judge concerning questions relating to compliance with international prescriptions. More recently, this tradition has weakened, and various steps have been taken to develop international institutions capable of providing authoritative judgments concerning alleged violations of such prescriptions. The International Court of Justice deals with issues of this type, and the United Nations itself has acquired some role in the application of the relevant prescriptions. It would be a serious error to overemphasize these developments; the Court is typically bypassed in important cases, and the decisions of the United Nations are frequently not accepted as authoritative. But the current situation certainly differs significantly from that obtaining in the nineteenth century (Rosenne, 1973). An important recent trend in this area concerns the authorization of individual members of the system to make applications of international prescriptions under well-defined conditions and according to agreed-upon standards. Such procedures are of course highly decentralized, but they differ fundamentally from the traditional arrangement based on unrestricted self-application. Arrangements

---

[15] For example, recent improvements in seismology make it increasingly possible to detect nuclear explosions without on-site inspection. And orbital satellites have dramatically reduced the chances of concealing a variety of military activities.

of this type are most appropriate with respect to highly iterative activities that occur within the territorial jurisdiction of individual actors. Developments along these lines have already occurred in connection with some of the commodity agreements (Fisher, 1971). And there are trends in this direction in such areas as the management of marine fisheries and the regulation of various forms of pollution (Burke, Legatski, and Woodhead, 1975).

The organization of sanctions at the international level has followed much the same course as the application of prescriptions (Doxey, 1971). The traditional system was based almost exclusively on the idea of unrestricted self-help. Each actor was authorized to respond in its own way to the alleged violations of others, subject only to the most general rules pertaining to appropriate responses (for example, the criterion of proportionality). Here too, the twentieth century has witnessed some efforts to introduce more centralized institutional arrangements. But these have been even less successful than similar efforts relating to the application of prescriptions, and it seems highly unlikely that significant centralizing tendencies will emerge during the foreseeable future. As in the case of the application of prescriptions, perhaps the most important trend concerns the gradual emergence of decentralized sanctioning processes. This trend involves authorizing individual members of the system to organize sanctions against violators on the basis of standards that are relatively well-defined and explicitly accepted by the community. Such arrangements may be accompanied by the development of more centralized agencies (for example, within the United Nations) designed to oversee and to coordinate the employment of sanctions by individual actors. Significant developments along these lines have already occurred in some functional areas, such as international air transport (Tauber, 1969). In other areas (for example, the control of marine pollution), there are good reasons to believe that we will experience increased movement in this direction (Yale Law Journal, 1973). In my judgment, the impact of this trend is likely to grow rather than to decline during the foreseeable future.

International externalities

What sorts of unintended side effects are generated by the highly decentralized systems of compliance mechanisms I have been describing in this section? At the level of the international system, it seems clear that it will not be necessary to worry about many of the types of negative externalities traditionally associated with the operation of compliance mechanisms. These externalities flow from the behavior of highly centralized public authorities, and there is nothing remotely resembling a set of institutions of this sort in the international system. But this does not mean that the problem of externalities can be ignored completely in thinking about compliance with international prescriptions.

The standard argument in this regard rests on the proposition that the international system is characterized by extensive ambiguity concerning the prevailing set of behavioral prescriptions and by generally low levels of compliance with those prescriptions. This, it is often argued, generates a variety of unintended by-products whose consequences are of far-reaching importance at the international level. These include such things as a generalized lack of predictability in the interactions among individual members of the system as well as a constant danger of escalating conflicts. In short, it is widely believed that many of the phenomena commonly associated with an uncooperative or even Hobbesian "state of nature" actually occur in the international system and that this situation is attributable to the absence of a more highly organized and centralized public authority.

I do not wish to assert that this line of reasoning is wholly without foundation. Nevertheless, I believe that it is seriously defective and that it overlooks some of the real virtues of highly decentralized social systems. To begin with, it is not at all clear that the level of compliance is strikingly low in the international system, although dramatic violations do occur with some frequency. On the contrary, it is a demonstrable fact that most acknowledged international prescriptions are complied with by the relevant actors most of the time. I shall have more to say about this matter in the succeeding chapters in which the problem of compliance with international prescriptions is investigated in greater depth through the use of case studies. Beyond this, it is well worth noting that decentralization at the level of the international system has important compensating virtues, even if it is conducive to the occurrence of costly violations from time to time. Not only is it true that the negative externalities associated with the operation of highly centralized public authorities are notably absent in this system. It is also true that the members of the international system have far more freedom than the members of most other social systems to develop autonomously and to establish their own preferences and priorities. Efforts to compare these compensating virtues with the costs of decentralization raise a normative issue that I cannot of course hope to resolve here. But there is no doubt in my mind that it would be a mistake to condemn the decentralized compliance mechanisms of the international system without examining carefully the benefits as well as the costs of this response to the problem of compliance.

PART II

Applications to international politics

CHAPTER 4

Compliance without organization: the Partial Nuclear Test Ban Treaty

As I have argued in the preceding chapters, the achievement of compliance does not always require the introduction of formal compliance mechanisms. It is not difficult to identify situations in which relatively high levels of compliance occur as a consequence of self-interest calculations, the impact of social pressures, or the effect of feelings of obligation. In this chapter, I want to explore these informal bases of compliance in the context of the international system. I have chosen the compliance system associated with the Partial Nuclear Test Ban Treaty as the vehicle for this exploration. This treaty deals with an issue in the realm of "high politics," a realm which many regard as a difficult one for the achievement of compliance. Though it is not the *most* critical issue relating to security in the contemporary world, the problem of nuclear testing is surely a significant one. Moreover, the test ban treaty has been in force long enough to make it a rich case for the study of compliance at the international level.

THE PARTIAL TEST BAN TREATY

The summer of 1963 witnessed the negotiation of two significant arms control agreements. The United States and the Soviet Union concluded the "hot line" agreement, a bilateral memorandum of understanding, on 20 June, 1963. Not requiring ratification, this agreement entered into force on the same day. Shortly thereafter, the Big Three reached agreement on a Partial Nuclear Test Ban Treaty. Final negotiations for this treaty began in Moscow on 15 July, 1963. It was finished on 25 July and signed by American, Soviet, and British representatives on 5 August. It entered into force on 10 October, 1963 upon deposit of ratifications by the United States, the Soviet Union, and Great Britain.

The Partial Test Ban Treaty (PTB) emerged from a protracted series of negotiations concerning the cessation of nuclear tests.[1] Proposals for a test ban go back as far as 1954. Active negotiations relating to this issue began in 1958 with the Conference of Experts (1 July to 21 August) and the opening of the Geneva Conference on 31 October, 1958. These developments were accompanied by the announcement of a voluntary moratorium on nuclear testing, which lasted from November 1958 until September 1961. Beginning in March 1962, negotiations for a ban on nuclear tests were carried forward within the framework of the Eighteen Nation Disarmament Conference meeting in Geneva. It is important to note, however, that prior to 1963 these negotiations focused primarily on the prospects of concluding a Comprehensive Test Ban Treaty (CTB). It is true that President Eisenhower suggested the possibility of a partial test ban as early as 1959 and that the United States tabled a draft treaty along these lines in August 1962. Nevertheless, it is clear that the idea of a partial test ban was treated as a distinctly secondary concern throughout most of the negotiations relating to the cessation of nuclear tests.

Despite the history of protracted negotiations in this realm, the actual test ban treaty was negotiated with great speed during the summer of 1963. The rapid pace of this development is generally attributed to the state of east-west relations in the wake of the Cuban missile crisis (SIPRI, 1973, p. 7). The missile crisis had placed a tremendous strain on Soviet-American relations and apparently impressed powerful leaders on both sides with the importance of taking steps to control the most serious dangers associated with the cold war. The Soviet side was also influenced at this time by the added incentives arising from the rapid deterioration of Sino-Soviet relations. And, since most responsible analysts on both sides regarded the partial test ban as self-enforcing, it was not necessary to become involved in protracted discussions about inspection and verification arrangements.

Formally, the PTB is a multilateral treaty among the United States, the Soviet Union, and Great Britain with provisions for accessions on the part of other members of the international community. The treaty must be ratified before it becomes binding on any state (SIPRI, 1973, p. 14). At the present time, 106 states are parties to the Partial Test Ban Treaty, the largest number of members for any international agreement relating to arms control or disarmament (SIPRI, 1976, pp. 427–468). Nevertheless, there are gaps of great importance in the membership. France, the People's Republic of China, Cuba, Saudi Arabia, and Vietnam have not acceded to the treaty in any form. In addition, Algeria, Argentina, Pakistan, and Portugal have failed to ratify the treaty even though they have signed it.

---

[1] For a thorough review see *World Armaments and Disarmament,* SIPRI Yearbook, (1972, pp. 389–469). The acronym SIPRI stands for Stockholm International Peace Research Institute.

Accordingly, the list of states not bound by the provisions of the treaty contains several nations with considerable nuclear potential as well as two nuclear-weapon states.

Though the PTB is an extremely brief document, it contains highly important provisions pertaining to amendment and withdrawal. Article II of the treaty states that any amendment ". . . must be approved by a majority of the votes of all the Parties to this Treaty, including the votes of all of the Original Parties." This means that the PTB can be altered with relative ease, so long as the United States, the Soviet Union, and Great Britain are in agreement concerning the terms of the proposed alteration.[2] Beyond this, while the treaty is formulated as an agreement of unlimited duration, it does explicitly allow for the possibility of withdrawal on the part of individual members. Thus, Article IV states that each member ". . . shall in exercising its national sovereignty have the right to withdraw from the Treaty if it decides that extraordinary events, related to the subject matter of this Treaty, have jeopardized the supreme interests of its country." Since the key elements of this provision are not formulated in operational terms, it is widely assumed that any member of the treaty can make its own decisions concerning the exact circumstances that would warrant withdrawal. The only limitation is that a withdrawing member must notify the other members of the treaty of its intention to withdraw three months in advance (SIPRI, 1973, pp. 14–19).

BEHAVIORAL PRESCRIPTIONS

It is often pointed out that the general objectives articulated in the preamble of the test ban treaty have not been fulfilled. The treaty has not led to an agreement on the cessation of all nuclear test explosions. Nor has it brought about the termination of the arms race.[3] Nevertheless, the PTB does contain three explicit prescriptions bearing directly on the behavior of the parties to the agreement.

Most important is the prescription prohibiting members from conducting nuclear explosions in three environments. This prescription, contained in Article I 1.(a), states that "Each of the Parties to this Treaty undertakes to prohibit, to prevent, and not to carry out any nuclear test explosion, or any other nuclear explosion, at any place under its jurisdiction or control: (a) in the atmosphere; beyond its limits, including outer space; or under water, including territorial waters or high seas." Note the sharp contrast between this provision and the central idea associated with proposals for a comprehensive test ban. Whereas a comprehensive ban would

[2] It also means that each of the Big Three has a *de facto* veto with respect to alterations in the test ban treaty (SIPRI, 1973, p. 14).

[3] Thus, the preamble speaks of efforts ". . . to achieve the discontinuance of all test explosions of nuclear weapons . . ." and calls for efforts ". . . to put an end to the armaments race . . ."

require the cessation of all nuclear explosions, the PTB explicitly permits members to continue conducting underground nuclear explosions.

The prohibition of all nuclear explosions and not just nuclear weapon test explosions in the three environments appears to preclude many potential programs involving peaceful uses of nuclear explosions. Also, it seems clear that the ban on explosions in outer space is meant to encompass nuclear explosions on celestial bodies, an interpretation confirmed by the Outer Space Treaty, which entered into force on 10 October, 1967.[4] At the same time, there are certain ambiguities associated with the exemption for underground explosions, because the meaning of the term "underground" is neither self-evident nor specified in operational terms in the text of the treaty. It is possible to argue that any explosion detonated beneath the surface of the earth, no matter how shallow, is permissible under the terms of the treaty. But a central purpose of the PTB is to curtail radioactive fallout, and nuclear explosions that are large and extremely shallow can produce substantial amounts of fallout. Under the circumstances, a more reasonable interpretation of this provision is that large, shallow explosions are permissible only if they do not introduce large quantities of radioactive products into the atmosphere. Finally, it should be noted that this first prescription of the PTB has been supplemented by the so-called Threshold Test Ban Treaty (TTBT) signed by the United States and the Soviet Union on 3 July, 1974. Briefly, this agreement specifies that nuclear weapon tests conducted underground are to be restricted to a maximum yield of 150 kilotons.[5]

The second behavioral prescription of the Partial Test Ban Treaty is contained in Article I 1.(b). This Article states that "Each of the Parties to this Treaty undertakes to prohibit, to prevent, and not to carry out any nuclear weapon test explosion, or any other nuclear explosion, at any place under its jurisdiction or control: (b) in any other environment if such explosion causes radioactive debris to be present outside the territorial limits of the State under whose jurisdiction or control such explosion is conducted." The purpose of this provision is to prohibit "venting" of underground explosions, at least when this involves the movement of radioactive debris across national boundaries. The underlying issue here is a relatively simple one. It sometimes happens that the force of an underground explosion causes the surface of the earth to crack. If these cracks are of significant size, radioactive products will escape through

---

[4] This treaty is formally entitled "A Treaty on Principles Governing the Activities of States in the Exploration and Use of Outer Space, including the Moon and Other Celestial Bodies."

[5] Formally, this is the "Treaty on the Limitation of Underground Nuclear Tests" (TTBT). It is a purely bilateral agreement between the United States and the Soviet Union; the agreement was supplemented by a "Treaty on Underground Nuclear Explosions for Peaceful Purposes" (PNE) signed by the same states on 28 May, 1976. For background information on the TTBT consult SIPRI (1975, pp. 405, 409).

them into the atmosphere. In fact, Article I 1.(b) does not proscribe such venting altogether. But it does prohibit venting when the escaping radioactive products cross any international frontier or national jurisdictional boundary. In the case of any given underground explosion, the likelihood of such an event occurring is a function of the following variables: the size of the explosion, the depth at which detonation occurs, the geographical location of the explosion, and the prevailing wind patterns in the area in question. Of course, the probability that some impermissible venting will occur can be expected to increase as a function of the number of underground explosions conducted.[6]

The last behavioral prescription of the PTB is contained in Article I 2. This Article states that "Each of the Parties to this Treaty, undertakes furthermore to refrain from causing, encouraging, or in any way participating in, the carrying out of any nuclear weapon test explosion, or any other nuclear explosion, anywhere which would take place in any of the environments described, or have the effect referred to, in paragraph 1 of the Article." The clear intent of this prohibition is to curtail tendencies toward the proliferation of nuclear weapons in the international system. This prescription differs from the other two in that it applies primarily to the existing nuclear weapon states or to states with a highly developed capability in the realm of nuclear energy. This is so because only these states are in a position actively to encourage or to participate in nuclear explosions on the part of others.

There is some ambiguity concerning the operational content of the prescription contained in Article I 2. There is no doubt that this provision prohibits deliberate or intentional assistance to nonnuclear states planning nuclear explosions other than those conducted underground. Nevertheless, the situation is much less clear with respect to the supply of fissionable materials and nuclear equipment (for example, power reactors or reprocessing facilities) to nonnuclear weapon states. This ambiguity arises from the following facts. The production of nuclear energy typically involves the creation of plutonium, which, of course can be used for the production of nuclear weapons. Moreover, there is no technical distinction, at least in the initial phases, between a testing program aimed at the development of nuclear devices for peaceful purposes and a testing program aimed at the production of nuclear weapons (SIPRI, 1975, pp. 16–37). Unless strict safeguards are imposed, it is possible for a nonnuclear weapon state to divert fissionable materials or nuclear equipment received for peaceful purposes into a weapons program. Presumably, this ambiguity in the PTB is clarified by the provisions of Article III.2 of the Non-Proliferation Treaty (NPT) of the 1968 (SIPRI, 1975, pp. 28–36), which make it permissible to supply fissionable materials and nuclear equipment to nonnuclear weapon states

[6] That is, states conducting extensive programs of underground testing must know that there is a high probability that some impermissible venting will occur.

only under relatively strict international safeguards operated by the International Atomic Energy Agency (IAEA).[7] Unfortunately, however, a number of important states (for example, Egypt, India, Israel) have refused to adhere to the NPT. Moreover, a considerable number of key states have so far failed to negotiate the details of the requisite safeguards agreements with the IAEA (SIPRI, 1975, pp. 34–35).

There has been a good deal of discussion about the significance of the prescriptions contained in the PTB.[8] The key question is whether any state has renounced anything of importance in agreeing to abide by the prescriptions incorporated in this treaty. Though it is not possible to answer this question definitively, a brief discussion of the issues at stake seems relevant at this juncture. To begin with, it is evident that some important or potentially important uses of nuclear explosions are not prohibited by the test ban treaty. During the course of the ratification process, it became quite clear that the Big Three did not intend the treaty to proscribe the use of nuclear weapons during war, even on a first-use basis (SIPRI, 1973, p. 9). Similarly, the PTB clearly permits underground explosions so long as they do not lead to violations of the prescription relating to venting. The implications of this are particularly important for the superpowers. While it is difficult and costly for other states to conduct underground explosions, it is possible for the superpowers to conduct a variety of nuclear weapon tests underground.

At the same time, the test ban treaty does prohibit a variety of activities that might otherwise seem attractive to certain states. It precludes some (but by no means all) tests relating to the development of active defense systems. It prohibits certain tests of weapons effects (for example, the impact of nuclear explosions on radar systems, hardened missile sites, and underwater installations). It rules out tests relating to the development of extremely high yield (100 megaton) devices. It severely complicates various tests directed toward the investigation of yield-to-weight ratios for nuclear weapons. And it prohibits all nuclear explosions for peaceful purposes except those that can be conducted underground and carried out without violating the terms of the prescription relating to venting. In addition, the PTB severely restricts the freedom of action of any nonnuclear weapon state which has adhered to the treaty but which acquires a pressing interest in developing operational nuclear weapons. One expert has gone so far as to assert that for a nonnuclear weapon state "To abjure atmos-

---

[7] Specifically, Article III.2 of the NPT states that ". . . parties undertake not to provide any non-nuclear-weapon state with (a) source or special fissionable (that is, any nuclear) material or (b) equipment or material 'especially designed for the processing, use or production of special fissionable material' unless that material shall be subject to 'the safeguards required by this article' " (SIPRI 1975, p. 30).

[8] See, for example, Jerome B. Wiesner and Herbert F. York, "National Security and the Nuclear Test Ban," and Eugene P. Wigner, "Commentary," in York (1973, pp. 129–136 and 137–139).

pheric testing is in effect to agree not to develop fission or fusion weapons" (York, 1973, p. 125). But virtually everyone would agree that adherence to the Partial Test Ban Treaty substantially inhibits the prospects of nuclear proliferation.

COMPLIANCE MECHANISMS

The Partial Test Ban Treaty is a remarkably brief document which contains no provisions at all for formally institutionalized compliance mechanisms (SIPRI, 1973, p. 12). Moreover, there was virtually no discussion of such mechanisms during the July 1963 negotiations in Moscow which led to the signing of the PTB. This is in marked contrast to the heavy emphasis on arrangements for inspection and verification during the protracted negotiations for a comprehensive test ban both before and after the signing of the PTB in 1963.[9]

There are several explanations for this deemphasis on formalized compliance mechanisms. To begin with, it is virtually impossible to engage in clandestine testing in the three environments on any significant scale (McNamara, 1963). Although some Americans expressed concern about the possibility of clandestine Soviet testing during the Senate debate on the test ban treaty in 1963, and there is a faint prospect that a single nuclear test could pass undetected if it were conducted in deep space, nevertheless, there is widespread agreement that no violator could carry out a meaningful series of nuclear tests without being detected (SIPRI, 1972, p. 415). Thus, elaborate inspection and verification procedures are unnecessary in conjunction with the partial test ban.[10]

At the same time, it was widely (though not universally) believed in 1963 that the principal parties to the Partial Test Ban Treaty would not experience strong incentives to violate the terms of the agreement (SIPRI, 1972, p. 410). In fact, as I shall argue in a later section of this chapter, there are both technical and political reasons why violations of the PTB are likely to look highly unattractive to most members.

It was also generally accepted in 1963 that any potential violator of the PTB would almost certainly exercise its option to withdraw from the treaty rather than attempting to violate the terms of the agreement

[9] Arrangements of this type have always constituted a key issue in negotiations involving proposals to establish a ban on (or even to restrict) underground explosions. The threshold test ban negotiated in 1974, for example, is accompanied by a detailed protocol dealing with inspection and verification procedures (SIPRI, 1975, p. 405).

[10] The area of impermissible venting may constitute a partial exception to this conclusion. Thus, ". . . the absence of an international control body evaluating events according to objective criteria set in advance makes it difficult to establish positive proof that radioactive substances from an underground nuclear explosion crossed the national boundaries of the testing country. An accused party could, therefore, easily deny the occurrence of prohibited leakages, especially if the detected amounts of radioactivity were not very significant" (SIPRI, 1973, pp. 12–13).

clandestinely.[11] As a carefully articulated SIPRI report puts it: "Any signatory nuclear-weapon nation that decided it needed to conduct further tests in these environments would probably use the escape clause rather than embark on secret tests; concealment would be extremely difficult, expensive and highly uncertain. Besides, these nations can realize nuclear weapon development by a programme of underground explosions; the prospective gains from atmospheric explosions are limited. If any other state party to the treaty decided to test, it would also prefer to act openly, rather than clandestinely, to demonstrate its capability to an enemy" (SIPRI, 1973, pp. 12–13).

It would be a serious mistake, however, to conclude from this discussion that no compliance mechanisms of any kind are operative in conjunction with the partial test ban. In fact, this case offers at least three illustrations of the important role of informal and noninstitutionalized compliance mechanisms with respect to behavioral prescriptions.

First, there is the discipline imposed by the phenomenon of reciprocity. It is generally accepted that significant violations on the part of other states would constitute legitimate grounds for any member of the agreement to exercise its option to withdraw, and there is every reason to believe that a withdrawal under such circumstances would shortly be followed by a resumption of testing on the part of the injured party.[12]

Any party engaging in violations would also have to reckon with the possibility that others would take retaliatory actions even without formally withdrawing from the treaty. Retaliation of this type might take the form of counter-violations designed to offset any advantages accruing to the original violator. But other retaliatory measures would also be open to the injured parties. These might take the form of military preparations, such as stepped up defense expenditures; economic sanctions, such as the abrogation of trade agreements; or political initiatives, such as official protests or the introduction of a resolution of censure in the United Nations. Contemplating the full range of possible retaliatory actions on the part of injured members, a potential violator might well think twice before initiating actions running directly counter to the terms of the test ban treaty.

Finally, it is important to consider the probable political repercussions of violations. There is no doubt that general opprobrium would fall on any state detected in significant violations of the terms of this treaty. For the nuclear weapon states, this would involve severe accusations of stimulating the arms race and breaking promises made to the nonnuclear weapon

---

[11] Henry P. Myers, "Extending the Nuclear Test Ban," in York (1973, p. 282).

[12] In order to ensure ratification of the treaty by the United States Senate, the Kennedy Administration proposed several safeguards designed to mitigate the criticisms of the treaty's opponents. One of these safeguards was a promise to maintain a capability to resume nuclear testing in the atmosphere on short notice (SIPRI, 1973, pp. 18–19).

states in the realm of arms control and disarmament.[13] For the nonnuclear weapon states, by contrast, this opprobrium would involve accusations of encouraging nuclear proliferation and behaving in a hypocritical fashion with respect to the problem of disarmament. In both cases, there is good reason to believe that the deterrent effect of these probable political repercussions is considerable.

THE RECORD

In formal terms, the record of compliance with the Partial Test Ban Treaty has been excellent to date, with a few exceptions relating to the problem of venting.[14] Compliance in this context compares favorably with the level of compliance achieved in other social systems. In domestic societies, for example, it is difficult to find prescriptions that are not violated significantly with some degree of frequency. At the same time, it seems helpful to distinguish between *pro forma* compliance and compliance with the spirit of an agreement. There are many cases in which it is possible to comply with the formal requirements of behavioral prescriptions even while acting in such a way that the achievement of the underlying purposes of the prescriptions is hindered. As I shall argue in this section, there are several areas in which members of the test ban agreement have engaged in activities running counter to the spirit of the treaty without formally violating the terms of the agreement.

Bearing these general comments in mind, let us examine the record associated with each of the specific behavioral prescriptions contained in the test ban treaty. No state adhering to the treaty has conducted a nuclear explosion in the atmosphere, in outer space, or underwater since the ratification of the treaty. In formal terms, therefore, the record of compliance with the first prescription of the treaty is perfect. Nevertheless, the United States and the Soviet Union have coupled formal compliance with large-scale increases in their programs of underground testing. As of 1974, for example, ". . . approximately half of the total of 1,012 nuclear explosions, conducted since 1945, were carried out after the conclusion of the PTBT" (SIPRI, 1975, p. 488). And one authority has spoken of ". . . what many believe is a nuclear-weapons development effort that is indistinguishable in scope—if it is not even larger—from the one that had been under way before the treaty."[15] It is apparent, then, that the test ban treaty has not resulted in an overall reduction in nuclear testing.

---

[13] The significance of this prospect is heightened by the fact that many nonnuclear weapon states already harbor strong feelings to the effect that the nuclear weapon states have failed to live up to their commitments in this realm.

[14] One authoritative source puts it this way: "The record of compliance with the treaty is generally considered good; there has been no complaint of a significant breach by any party" (SIPRI, 1973, p. 21).

[15] Henry P. Myers, "Extending the Nuclear Test Ban," in York (1973, p. 293).

The other two nuclear weapon states, France and China, have not formally adhered to the PTB. It is consequently possible for these states to argue that the terms of this agreement are irrelevant to their nuclear testing programs.[16] These two states conducted fifty-three nuclear explosions during the period 1963–1973, forty-five of them in the atmosphere. Though these efforts do not constitute formal violations of the PTB, they certainly flout the underlying spirit of the treaty. The nonnuclear weapon states have also formally complied with the terms of this prescription. Nevertheless, several of these states have engaged in activities that are not easy to square with the spirit of the prescription. India, for example, conducted an underground explosion with a yield of 12 kilotons on 8 May, 1974 (SIPRI, 1975, pp. 16–19). Similarly, it is widely believed that several other states (for example, Israel) have undertaken nuclear developments of military significance, though these developments have not resulted in actual explosions (SIPRI, 1975, pp. 22–28). None of these activities constitutes a formal violation of the first prescription of the PTB, but they are certainly not reassuring from the point of view of efforts to make progress toward the achievement of the general objectives articulated in the preamble of the treaty.

The record associated with the second prescription contained in the PTB is a considerably different one. To begin with, ". . . almost every underground explosion releases some radioactive products into the atmosphere, which may pass over the border, and which may or may not be detected. The question which remains unanswered in the PTB is just what would constitute a violation; just any amount or a dangerous amount of radioactive products" (SIPRI, 1973, p. 11). Moreover, there have in fact been a number of cases in which significant amounts of radioactive debris from underground tests have been identified crossing international jurisdictional boundaries (Gillette, 1974). "Approximately a dozen nuclear tests conducted by the Soviet Union since August 1963 have vented radioactivity into the atmosphere and across Soviet borders in northern Europe and the Far East. Two or three U.S. tests have also released radioactive fallout over the Canadian and Mexican borders" (SIPRI, 1975, p. 488).

In actuality, these cases of venting have been deemphasized diplomatically by both sides and treated as mere "technical" violations of the PTB (SIPRI, 1973, p. 11). This is no doubt a highly significant indicator of the mutual interest of the superpowers in maintaining the basic viability of the test ban treaty and avoiding the political repercussions that would flow from its disruption. But what is the formal status of these venting incidents?

---

[16] This is clearly true if we accept the view that the terms of international agreements and treaties are only relevant to states that consent to them explicitly. There is an alternative view, held by some students of international law, which suggests that agreements subscribed to by the overwhelming majority of states are applicable to all members of the international community. Actual experience with the test ban treaty does not lend much support to this alternative view.

From the point of view of compliance, is there an important distinction between technical violations and substantive violations? It is difficult to avoid the conclusion that these incidents must be classified as definite violations of the terms of the treaty (SIPRI, 1975, p. 488). Although it is possible to emphasize the relatively small amounts of radioactive debris involved, the language of the treaty offers scant support for the proposition that low levels of venting are permissible. Similarly, it is difficult to maintain that the occurrence of these cases of venting was altogether unintended or unforeseeable. In connection with extensive programs of underground testing, the probability that some venting will take place in violation of the terms of the PTB is extremely high.[17] At the same time, it would undoubtedly be a mistake to make too much of these cases of venting in this discussion of compliance with the test ban. Though they must be treated formally as violations, they have certainly not destroyed the overall viability of the treaty regime and they are undoubtedly less significant than other developments in the nuclear realm which are not formally violations of the PTB.

An evaluation of the record with respect to the third prescription raises yet another range of questions. As far as intentional or deliberate violations of this prescription are concerned, the record of compliance is excellent. No nonnuclear state adhering to the test ban has conducted a nuclear explosion in the three environments, a fact that constitutes *prima facie* evidence of compliance with this prescription. Moreover, there is no evidence of any member of the PTB deliberately encouraging a nonnuclear weapon state to take steps toward the achievement of a nuclear capability. The only remotely questionable case stems from the position of Canada vis-à-vis the Indian nuclear explosion of May 1974 (SIPRI, 1975, p. 21). Since that explosion was conducted underground and since the Canadian government expressed obvious dismay at the occurrence of the explosion, there is no real basis for concluding that prior Canadian nuclear assistance to India constituted a violation of prescription no. 3 of the PTB. But this case does illustrate the inherent ambiguities lurking in this area. As a recent SIPRI report puts it, "The Indian nuclear explosion brought about a wider realization of the fact that the present availability of nuclear technology and fissionable material aggravates the possibility of nuclear weapon proliferation." (SIPRI, 1975, p. 496).

Beyond this, there is a confusing twilight zone that makes it difficult to evaluate compliance with the prescription. Numerous members of the treaty have supplied fissionable material or nuclear equipment to other countries under the terms of a variety of agreements (SIPRI, 1975, pp. 22–37). In the light of the discussion in a previous section concerning the difficulty of differentiating objectively among various types of nuclear pro-

[17] This is especially true in the case of programs, like those of the United States and the Soviet Union, which include large underground explosions (over ½ megaton).

grams, do these forms of nuclear assistance violate either the letter or the spirit of the test ban treaty? The ultimate answer to this question depends on the intentions of the various parties involved. But intentions are notoriously difficult to evaluate objectively, especially in social systems in which actors often experience powerful incentives not to reveal them. All this makes it difficult to reach definitive conclusions concerning the record of compliance with this prescription. Nevertheless, it seems reasonable to offer the following formulation. When nuclear materials and equipment are supplied to nonnuclear weapon states within the framework of the system of safeguards outlined in the Non-Proliferation Treaty (NPT), such assistance should be viewed as compatible with the terms of the test ban treaty (SIPRI, 1975, pp. 22–37). When such materials and equipment are deliberately supplied outside the framework of these safeguards, on the other hand, there should be some presumption that the activities in question constitute violations of the terms of the PTB. That is, states offering nuclear assistance outside this system of safeguards should be called upon to show why these activities do not violate the terms of the PTB. If this formulation is accepted, it is necessary to conclude that a number of states are currently engaging in activities that are at least questionable under the terms of the test ban. A prominent case in point stems from the pledges of nuclear assistance which the United States made to Egypt and Israel in 1974 (SIPRI, 1975, pp. 34–37).

What can we say by way of conclusion concerning the record of compliance with the test ban treaty? It is certainly true that various members have violated the spirit of this agreement from time to time. Nevertheless, perhaps the most important point to emphasize is that the PTB has survived all the ups and downs of world politics since 1963 without losing its essential viability or its symbolic significance. Specifically, it has survived the strains arising from the Dominican intervention of 1965 and the Czech intervention of 1968, the Sino-Soviet rift, the Vietnam war, the Indo-Pakistani wars of 1965 and 1971, and the Middle East wars of 1967 and 1973. This is a notable achievement, especially in the absence of any formalized compliance mechanisms. At a minimum, it demonstrates that it is not impossible for behavioral prescriptions to remain fundamentally viable even in such highly decentralized and volatile social systems as the international system.

ANALYSIS

How can we account for the relatively impressive record of compliance with the partial test ban described in the preceding section? Of course, it is not possible to provide a definitive answer to this question. Nevertheless, the general picture seems clear.

Consider first the behavior of the nuclear weapon states adhering to the PTB (that is, the United States, the Soviet Union, and Great Britain). It is extremely doubtful whether any one of these states could benefit significantly from violating the treaty, even if such violations did not lead to the collapse of the test ban regime (SIPRI, 1972, p. 417). None of these states is likely to experience compelling incentives to conduct nuclear tests in response to presumed clandestine testing by the others since serious clandestine testing in the three environments is virtually impossible, as I indicated earlier. The contrast between this situation and the one that would arise under the terms of a comprehensive test ban is worth noting.[18] Next, each of these states can deal with a large majority of any presumed military needs for nuclear testing by conducting underground explosions. Beyond this, it is widely acknowledged that the incentives for the super-powers to conduct nuclear weapon tests have declined substantially since the ratification of the test ban treaty. This is due primarily to the facts that it is hard to foresee any major breakthroughs relating directly to nuclear explosions and that the most important prospects for technological advances with direct military applications do not require nuclear weapon tests (McNamara, 1963). Finally, there is little doubt that the strategic balance between the superpowers has become more and more insensitive to any plausible developments in nuclear technology in recent years. As one authority puts it, ". . . the advanced status of nuclear-weapons de-velopment, the existence of very large weapons stockpiles and the deter-rent value of the ability to destroy even one city suggest that neither the continuation of nuclear-weapon tests nor the cessation of such tests will affect the strategic position of one superpower with respect to the other."[19] In short, none of the original parties to the test ban has much to gain from a policy of conducting nuclear explosions in violation of the terms of the treaty.

At the same time, violations of the PTB would impose substantial costs on any one of these states. Though some of these costs would be intangi-ble and difficult to measure precisely, they would certainly not be negli-gible. In the first instance, such violations would generate widespread political opprobrium and charges of hypocrisy. Many nonnuclear weapon states already feel that the test ban treaty is a highly discriminatory agree-ment. Violations of the treaty on the part of one or more of the Big Three would undoubtedly produce much greater feelings of alienation on the part of numerous nonnuclear weapon states. Therefore, violations on the part of one of the superpowers could be expected to have a significant negative impact on the prospects of that state in the east-west competition for sup-port and allegiance in the nonaligned world. Similarly, clear-cut violations of the PTB would almost certainly disrupt decisively the momentum to-ward further arms control agreements desired by both superpowers. In

---

[18] Given recent developments in the field of seismology, it is extremely doubtful whether any state could successfully conduct a program of clandestine testing even under the terms of a comprehensive test ban treaty. Nevertheless, fears relating to clandestine testing under a comprehensive test ban remain widespread in certain quarters.

[19] Henry P. Myers, "Extending the Nuclear Test Ban," in York (1973, pp. 292–293).

fact, the test ban treaty has been followed by the negotiation of additional arms control agreements of some importance (for example, the Outer Space Treaty, the NPT, and SALT I). Major violations of the test ban treaty would severely undermine this series of negotiations. More generally, it is probable that major violations would have a substantial destabilizing impact on east-west relations and constitute a severe blow to the so-called détente between the superpowers. There is every indication that both the western powers and the Soviet Union would regard this as a high price to pay for any gains that could be reaped from such violations.

The cases of France and China illustrate another key feature of compliance with the Partial Test Ban Treaty. The fact that these states have refused to adhere to the treaty emphasizes the point that those actors who would be most likely to become violators if they had adhered to the treaty have refused even to accept the behavioral prescriptions contained in it. Once again, this exemplifies an important difference between many prescriptions in the international system and those in many other social systems discussed in the preceding chapter.[20] Moreover, this fact undoubtedly serves to make the impressive level of compliance with the PTB somewhat less remarkable.

Consider finally the behavior of the other states adhering to the test ban treaty. The first thing to notice is that the great majority of these states have no compelling incentives to go nuclear or to conduct nuclear explosions in violation of the partial test ban. The costs of such a policy would be exorbitant for most states, and the dangers of provoking further nuclear proliferation would more than offset any security gains that might be realized. Accordingly, the idea of violating the PTB is a rather academic question for most of the nonnuclear weapon states. In any case, however, the partial test ban also leaves considerable scope for nuclear development on the part of nonnuclear weapon states. Underground explosions are permissible under the terms of the treaty. India's underground explosion in 1974 does not appear to have violated any of the explicit prescriptions of the PTB.[21] In addition, it is now clear that it is possible to achieve nuclear developments having considerable military significance without conducting any nuclear explosions at all. Though this is more controversial, there may even be cases in which the diplomatic-strategic advantages flowing from such developments approach those that would emanate from the conduct of a few nuclear explosions.[22]

---

[20] That is, many international prescriptions are applicable only to subjects consenting to them explicitly. Prescriptions in other social systems often apply to entire groups regardless of whether individual members of these groups have consented to them explicitly.

[21] It did not, for example, generate any significant venting (SIPRI, 1975, pp. 16–19).

[22] For example, it is often argued that the deterrent effect of Israel's recent developments in the nuclear realm is essentially as great as could be obtained from conducting an actual nuclear explosion. For a contrary view, however, see SIPRI, 1972, pp. 423.

Beyond this, there are important political factors inducing the nonnuclear weapon states to refrain from violations of the test ban treaty. Clear violations of the PTB would almost certainly produce strong negative reactions from one or both of the superpowers. In fact, the United States and the Soviet Union might well join forces in condemning any other member of the PTB engaging in such violations. Furthermore, many nonnuclear weapon states have a well-developed desire to exercise some political influence in the realm of arms control and disarmament by acting in an exemplary fashion with regard to nuclear technology. There can be no doubt whatsoever that major violations of the treaty would severely undermine efforts on the part of the nonnuclear weapon states to bring pressure to bear on the superpowers on the basis of arguments relating to equity and the fulfillment of promises.

CONCLUSION

In concluding this chapter, it seems appropriate to inquire about the implications of this discussion of the Partial Nuclear Test Ban Treaty for the study of compliance in general. Though it would be a mistake to generalize facilely from a single case such as this, a few observations along these lines are pertinent. Above all, this case suggests that viable behavioral prescriptions are not only feasible in highly decentralized social systems like the international system; high levels of compliance are possible as well. It is undoubtedly right to assert that "No arms control treaty can completely rule out the possibility of evasion; all it can do is to minimize its probability" (SIPRI, 1974, p. 387). However, it is noteworthy that the actual record of compliance with the PTB is impressive, even by comparison with compliance records in far more centralized domestic systems.

The case of the test ban treaty also makes it clear that the achievement of compliance in highly decentralized social systems is possible in the absence of formalized compliance mechanisms and certainly in the absence of elaborate enforcement procedures. It would not do to conclude from this that the problem of compliance is relatively easy to solve in decentralized systems, but this evidence does disconfirm any proposition to the effect that the presence of enforcement capabilities is a necessary condition for the achievement of compliance.

Further, this study of the test ban treaty suggests that there is an important role for informal compliance mechanisms in highly decentralized social systems; informal mechanisms of various types are no doubt of great significance in other social systems as well. Informal compliance mechanisms may prove just as effective as more formalized arrangements, especially in cases where the direct self-interest calculations of the actors serve to sustain the behavioral prescriptions in question. There is little doubt that some such process is a central factor in the achievement of relatively high levels of compliance with the prescriptions contained in the PTB. And there is no reason to conclude that the test ban treaty is unusual or atypical in this respect.

Finally, a note of caution seems appropriate. It is important not to exaggerate or to inflate the lessons of this case. In fact, the PTB has certain characteristics that facilitate the achievement of compliance and that cannot be counted upon to be present in all cases. It is easy to detect any serious violations of the test ban treaty without introducing elaborate and highly institutionalized arrangements for inspection and verification. In this connection, there is a striking contrast between the PTB and a comprehensive test ban or even the Threshold Test Ban Treaty negotiated in 1974 (SIPRI, 1975, p. 405). In addition, most members of the test ban treaty do not have strong incentives to engage in violations of the agreement. Compliance does not prevent members from pursuing most of their key objectives, and the costs associated with major violations would be substantial. Beyond this, there is the fact that major violations of the PTB would have far-reaching political repercussions due to the symbolic significance of this agreement in contemporary world politics. Consequently, violators cannot hope to engage in obscure (though detected) violations in connection with this treaty. These comments on the special features of the PTB should not be allowed to detract from the fact that the record of compliance with the prescriptions incorporated in this treaty has been excellent to date. But they do illustrate the dangers involved in generalizing too facilely from a single case such as this.

CHAPTER 5

Decentralized institutions: the International North Pacific Fisheries Convention

As I indicated in chapter 3, there is no centralized and formally organized public authority in the international system. Although this might lead us to ignore or deemphasize the role of institutionalized compliance mechanisms in this sociopolitical system, it would be a mistake to do so. In this chapter, I want to examine in some depth the operation of decentralized institutions in efforts to achieve compliance in the international system. I have chosen a compliance system associated with the marine fisheries of the North Pacific as a vehicle for this examination. The pertinent prescriptions deal with the international relations of resource management, a topic of growing importance in the contemporary world. The decentralized institutions introduced in conjunction with this compliance system are sufficiently complex to illustrate a variety of aspects of decentralized compliance mechanisms. And the institutions in question have been in existence long enough to make this case a rich one for this study.[1]

[1] This case study draws heavily on a series of discussions I held during the spring of 1977 in the Pacific Northwest, Canada, and Alaska. Though I shall not attribute specific conclusions to single individuals, these discussions were of great importance in shaping my analysis of the INPFC. Those whose comments were particularly helpful include: Donald McKernan of the Institute of Marine Studies at the University of Washington; Dayton L. Alverson of the Northwest and Alaska Fisheries Center of the National Marine Fisheries Service; Norman Wilimovsky of the Institute of Animal Resource Ecology at the University of British Columbia; Toshio Isogai, executive director of the International North Pacific Fisheries Commission; C. R. Forester, assistant director of the International North Pacific Fisheries Commission; W. R. Hourston of the Canadian Department of the Environment; Bruce Leaman of the Pacific Biological Station at Nanaimo; Ronald Naab of the National Marine Fisheries Service in Juneau; Admiral John Hayes, commandant of the United States Coast Guard 17th District in Juneau; Commander Ralph Giffin of the United States Coast Guard 17th District in Juneau; Charles Meacham of the office of the governor of the state of

THE INTERNATIONAL NORTH PACIFIC FISHERIES CONVENTION

On 9 May, 1952, the United States, Canada, and Japan signed the International Convention for the High Seas Fisheries of the North Pacific Ocean (commonly known as the International North Pacific Fisheries Convention or INPFC). The three states exchanged ratifications of the Convention in Tokyo on 12 June, 1953, thereby bringing the agreement formally into force. During the intervening years, the INPFC has remained the principal international agreement relating to the high seas fisheries of the North Pacific.[2]

The International North Pacific Fisheries Convention arose from a widespread desire to resolve various issues remaining from World War II. Specifically, it emerged as an element in the move to normalize relations between Japan and the western allied powers during the early 1950s (the general Japanese Peace Treaty, signed in San Francisco on 8 September, 1951, entered into force on 28 April, 1952). The essential purpose of negotiating the Convention was to facilitate the development of Japanese high seas fisheries in the North Pacific, while at the same time providing a measure of protection for certain stocks of marine fish of North American origin (Copes, 1976, pp. 6–8). The importance of this objective for Japan was heightened by the closure of traditional fishing areas off the coast of Kamchatka and the Kurile Islands, over and above the general disruption of Japanese high seas fishing operations caused by the war.[3] As the dominant participant in the negotiations, however, the United States played the leading role in formulating the specific terms of the Convention.

The INPFC establishes a three-nation regime designed ". . . to ensure the maximum sustained productivity of the fishery resources of the North Pacific Ocean" (Preamble).[4] The Convention area extends to ". . . all

---

Alaska; Edward Huizer, deputy commissioner of the Alaska Department of Fish and Game; William Smoker, director of the Auke Bay laboratory of the National Marine Fisheries Service; Eugene Buck of the Arctic Environmental Information and Data Center in Anchorage; James Branson, executive director of the North Pacific Fisheries Council, and Walter Parker, state co-chairman of the Joint Federal-State Land Use Planning Commission in Anchorage.

[2] It is not, however, the only significant international agreement affecting this region. Others of particular note include: the Convention for the Protection, Preservation, and Extension of the Sockeye Salmon Fishery of the Fraser River System (negotiated by the United States and Canada in 1930 and amended to include pink salmon in 1956); the Convention between the United States and Canada for the Preservation of the Halibut Fisheries of the North Pacific Ocean (negotiated in 1923 and renegotiated in 1930, 1937, and 1953), and the Soviet-Japanese Convention on the High Seas Fisheries of the Northwest Pacific Ocean (negotiated in 1956).

[3] The Kuriles passed into Soviet hands at the end of World War II. At the time, the Soviets showed little inclination to permit the resumption of prewar Japanese fishing activities in the area around Kamchatka.

[4] The INPFC is a product of the era in which the principle of maximum sustained yield was influential. On the more recent fate of this principle see Larkin (1977).

waters, other than territorial waters, of the North Pacific Ocean which for the purposes hereof shall include the adjacent seas" [Article I(1)]. The Contracting Parties, the United States, Canada, and Japan, were the only states with well-developed interests in the marine fisheries of this region in 1952. The growth of high seas fishing operations in the North Pacific by noncontracting parties in recent years (for example, the Soviet Union, Korea, and Poland) has produced serious difficulties for the INPFC regime (Chitwood, 1969). Though there is nothing in the Convention itself that would preclude the extension of the regime to these additional states, it has not proven politically feasible to move in this direction.

Formally, the INPFC is a multilateral convention requiring ratification through the constitutional processes of the Contracting Parties as well as an exchange of instruments of ratification. Acceptance of the terms of the agreement therefore can be regarded as a form of explicit consent on the part of the members of the regime. The Contracting Parties agree to maintain the agreement in force for a period of at least ten years. Thereafter, the Convention will remain in force ". . . until one year from the day on which a Contracting Party shall give notice . . . of an intention of terminating the Convention" [Article XI(2)]. The Convention itself does not contain explicit provisions relating to amendments or alterations of the terms of the agreement. It seems reasonable to infer, however, that at least some substantive issues can be dealt with through the passage of resolutions as provided for in Article II(3). More fundamental changes in the character of the regime would undoubtedly require a general renegotiation of the terms of the Convention.

The INPFC establishes a permanent Commission in addition to a set of substantive rules or prescriptions.[5] The Commission is accorded certain functions in the realms of research and the formulation of recommendations to the Contracting Parties concerning harvesting practices and conservation measures (Article III), but it has no real staff of its own, and authority relating to important matters is reserved to the Contracting Parties.[6] Consequently, the Commission of the INPFC can hardly be regarded as a well-developed public authority, as that concept is employed in this study.

Recent developments have raised fundamental questions about the future of the INPFC. In essence, these developments stem from the expansion of coastal state jurisdictions over marine fisheries. A pronounced trend in this direction has emerged in recent years in conjunction with the Third Law

[5] Thus, Article II(2) states that "The Commission shall be composed of three national sections, each consisting of not more than four members appointed by the governments of the respective Contracting Parties."

[6] Compare this situation with that arising under the Fraser River Salmon Convention or the Halibut Convention, each of which establishes a commission with an independent staff.

of the Sea Conference under the auspices of the United Nations. With respect to the Convention area of the INPFC, this shift has been formalized
through the unilateral promulgation of 200-mile fisheries jurisdictions by
Canada (1 January, 1977) and the United States (1 March, 1977).[7] The
United States has also advanced far-reaching jurisdictional claims relating
to the anadromous species of the North Pacific.[8] The consequences of
these developments for the INPFC regime are obvious and extensive. They
undermine the rules regarding the harvest of fish outlined in the Convention (more on these rules later), and they imply a need for major adjust-
ments of conservation measures in the Convention area. On 10 February,
1977, therefore, the United States informed the other Contracting Parties
of its intention to terminate the Convention. This step was clearly meant
more as a forceful sign of an American determination to renegotiate the
terms of the agreement than as an indicator of a decision to discard the
INPFC altogether. The ensuing negotiations produced a Protocol to the
original Convention, signed in Tokyo on 25 April, 1978. In essence, this
Protocol (1) commits Japan to accepting the extended managerial authority of the United States and Canada in the new fishery conservation zones
and (2) redefines the times and areas in which Japanese vessels are
permitted to operate in the high seas salmon fisheries of the North Pacific.

The regime that is emerging from these developments will differ drastically from the arrangements set forth in the 1952 Convention, though
something called the INPWC will continue in existence. But it is too
early to tell just how this new regime will work out in practice. Accordingly, I shall focus on the compliance system articulated in the 1952
Convention. In a sense, then, this chapter offers an analysis of a completed
case. Nonetheless, because the future of the INPFC remains unclear and
because it facilitates exposition, I shall generally use the present tense in
discussing the operation of the INPFC regime.

BEHAVIORAL PRESCRIPTIONS

The INPFC establishes a general regime for the marine fisheries of the
North Pacific. It outlines arrangements for the conduct of research and
formulates procedures for adding new prescriptions as well as modifying
existing ones. At the same time, however, the Convention itself spells out
a number of explicit prescriptions applicable to the behavior of the Contracting Parties. Some of them proscribe certain actions, while others call
upon specified parties to undertake positive measures. It is these explicit

---

[7] In the Canadian case, this step was taken under the provisions of the Territorial Sea
and Fishing Zones Act. For the United States, the relevant legislation is the Fishery Conservation and Management Act of 1976 (PL 94-265).

[8] See Section 102 of the Fishery Conservation and Management Act, which claims
exclusive fishery management authority over "All anadromous species throughout the
migratory range of each such species beyond the fishery conservation zone . . ."

behavioral prescriptions of the INPFC which I shall focus on in this case study.

First, the Convention introduces the so-called abstention principle, which provides for abstention from efforts to exploit certain stocks of fish by some member nations ". . . where it can be shown that, historically, these have not fished the stock—and that the other member nations are fully utilizing the resource and have it under study and scientific management" (Naab, 1969, p. 49). While the Convention articulates several conditions necessary for the abstention principle to apply [Article IV(1)(b)], experience has shown that there is room for considerable disagreement in applying these conditions to concrete cases.[9] Under the terms of the INPFC, the principle of abstention applies primarily to the activities of Japanese fishermen, but it extends to certain activities on the part of Canadian operators as well. Three major abstention rules are spelled out in an Annex to the Convention: for salmon, halibut, and herring. Each of these rules requires brief comment here.

The rule pertaining to salmon constitutes the critical case both because of the complexity of the population dynamics of salmon stocks and because of the economic importance of the salmon fisheries (Haig-Brown, 1967). It applies to all five commercially significant species of North Pacific salmon (that is, sockeye, pink, coho, chum, and chinook). Both Japan and Canada agree to abstain from fishing for salmon in the Bering Sea east of a line running generally along 175° West Longitude.[10] In the Convention area to the south of the Bering Sea, Japan (but not Canada) agrees to refrain from fishing for salmon east of 175° W. Several points relating to this abstention line are worthy of comment. First, the line has been a source of continuing problems and complaints. It is impossible to manage stocks of marine fish coherently with reference to a precise line because the migratory habits of the fish in question are simply not sufficiently regular. In addition, while there is some evidence to indicate that the line at 175° W was originally fixed with the idea of protecting virtually all stocks of salmon of North American origin from exploitation by Japanese fishermen, the arrangement has not led to the achievement of this goal. It is now clear that significant numbers of salmon of North American origin migrate past 175° W, particularly in the northern portions of the Convention area (Haig-Brown, 1967, p. 28). And the

---

[9] The conditions of Article IV are: (1) that the stock is being fully utilized, (2) that the stock is subject to regulation by those exploiting it, and (3) that the stock is being studied scientifically.

[10] The precise formulation in Annex (2) refers to "The Convention area of the Bering Sea east of the line starting from Cape Prince of Wales on the west coast of Alaska, running westward to 168°58'22.59" West Longitude; thence due south to a point 65°15'00" North Latitude; thence along the great circle course which passes through 51° North Latitude and 167° East Longitude, to its intersection with meridian 175° West Longitude; thence south along a provisional line which follows this meridian to the territorial waters limit of Atka Island . . ."

Japanese have been able to harvest a good many of these fish without formally violating the abstention line in any way.[11] In fact, a Protocol to the original Convention emphasizes that the line at 175° W is to be treated only as a provisional line and sets forth a procedure for modifying it under certain conditions. In the intervening years, however, efforts to reach agreement on alterations of the provisional line have proven fruitless, so that the original provision of the Convention has remained in operation by default.

The case of halibut is more straightforward, at least as formulated in the Convention. At the outset, Japan simply agreed to refrain from fishing for halibut of North American origin in ". . . the Convention area off the coasts of Canada and the United States of America in which commercial fishing for halibut is being or can be prosecuted" [Annex (1)(a)]. After a protracted debate, this rule was modified in 1963 in order to exclude the Bering Sea from the abstention area for Japanese fishermen. This debate turned on the question of the extent to which the halibut stocks of the Bering Sea were being fully utilized by North American fishermen, a condition regarded as necessary to justify the continuation of Japanese abstention under the terms of Article IV of the Convention.[12] Apart from this, it is pertinent to note that the abstention rule for halibut has not been construed to prohibit Japanese trawling operations for other species of groundfish, even though these operations pick up significant numbers of halibut as an incidental catch.

The remaining abstention rule outlined in the Annex relates to herring. Originally, Japan agreed to refrain from harvesting herring throughout the Convention area except in the Bering Sea and in ". . . the waters of the North Pacific Ocean west of the meridian passing through the extremity of the Alaskan Peninsula . . ." [Annex (1)(b)]. But the Japanese gradually succeeded in persuading the Americans and the Canadians to accept the conclusion that not all of the herring stocks of this zone are qualified for abstention under the terms of Article IV of the Convention. Under the circumstances, a series of amendments to the Annex (in 1960, 1962, and 1963) reduced the area of Japanese abstention with respect to herring

[11] Pertinent data on this harvest are displayed in the U.S. Final Preliminary Management Plans for the High Seas Fisheries of Japan prepared under the supervision of the North Pacific Fisheries Council. Harvesting salmon on the high seas is generally regarded as inefficient. This is so because: (1) individual fish continue to gain weight until their return to fresh water, (2) it is easier to capture salmon at the mouths of spawning streams than on the high seas, and (3) there is more opportunity to make last minute judgments concerning escapement to maintain the stocks when fish are harvested as they return to the spawning streams. Nevertheless, none of this makes the Japanese practice of harvesting salmon of North American origin beyond 175° W incompatible with the terms of the INPFC.

[12] Many commentators argue that subsequent experience has demonstrated that the 1963 amendment to the Annex provision on halibut was unwise.

to a relatively small zone off the Canadian coast around the Queen Charlotte Islands.[13] The current abstention rule for herring, therefore, is far less restrictive than that originally set forth in the Annex.

Additions to the abstention rules outlined in the Annex would be quite possible under the terms of the INPFC [Articles II(3) and III(1)(b)]. In fact, the Convention envisions a continuous process of review and adjustment in this realm.[14] But no such additions were agreed to by the Contracting Parties during the years 1953–1978. In effect, the abstention principle has proven to be a nonextendable concept, at least in the context of the three-nation regime for the North Pacific. On the other hand, the INPFC has provided a forum for the negotiation of several bilateral agreements involving ideas analogous to abstention.[15] Though these agreements cannot be construed as extensions of the INPFC regime in any strict sense, some commentators regard the development of this negotiating forum as one of the more notable achievements of the INPFC regime.

The behavioral prescriptions of the INPFC are not confined to the system of abstention rules summarized in the preceding paragraphs. The next most important prescription is that pertaining to conservation measures [Articles V(2), IX(1)(b), and Annex]. In an important sense, this prescription constitutes the opposite side of the coin of the abstention principle. The duty to develop and implement an effective program of conservation measures for the relevant stocks is conceptualized explicitly as a concomitant of the right to harvest these stocks.

Contracting Parties participating in the harvest of stocks of fish regulated under the terms of the INPFC agree to ". . . continue to carry out necessary conservation measures" [Article V(2)]. It is clear that this is a positive prescription aimed primarily at the United States and Canada.[16] But the exact requirements of the prescription are not spelled out clearly in the

[13] Annex (1)(b) now refers to "The Convention area off the coast of Canada in which commercial fishing for herring of Canadian origin is being or can be prosecuted, exclusive of the waters of the high seas north of 51°56′ North Latitude and west of the Queen Charlotte Islands and west of a line drawn between Langara Point on Langara Island, Queen Charlotte Islands, and Cape Muzon on Dall Island in southeast Alaska."

[14] Thus, Article III(1)(b) includes the following statement in its enumeration of the functions of the Commission: "To permit later additions to the Annex, study, on request of a Contracting Party, any stock of Fish of the Convention area, the greater part of which is harvested by one or more of the Contracting Parties, for the purpose of determining whether such stock qualifies for abstention under the provisions of Article IV."

[15] The most important of these are the following agreements between the United States and Japan: (1) an agreement regarding the king and tanner crab fisheries in the eastern Bering Sea (1974); (2) an agreement concerning the fisheries off the coast of the United States (1974); and (3) an agreement relating to the salmon fisheries in waters contiguous to the United States territorial sea (1974).

[16] It has some important implications for Japan as well, due to the fact that the abstention line at 175° W permits Japanese fishermen to participate in the harvest of salmon in the Convention area.

Convention. For example, while the typical formula enjoins the relevant Contracting Parties to "continue" to carry out conservation measures, the Convention also implies that new conservation measures should be developed and implemented from time to time [Article III(1)(c)]. Again, the Convention clearly anticipates that joint conservation measures will be important with regard to the relevant stocks,[17] but it certainly does not commit the Contracting Parties to embrace joint conservation measures in any particular case. Similarly, Article III outlines an important role for the Commission in conducting research relevant to conservation and formulating specific conservation measures for recommendation to the Contracting Parties. But effective authority relating to the adoption of such measures is clearly retained by the Contracting Parties, and there is no implication that they will generally respond favorably to recommendations developed by the Commission. All this is not to suggest that the prescription of the INPFC pertaining to conservation measures is unimportant. But it does make clear that there is room for considerable disagreement concerning its operational content.

A supplementary prescription of the INPFC deals with information gathering and the conduct of research. Thus, Article VIII states that the ". . . Contracting Parties agree to keep as far as practicable all records requested by the Commission and to furnish compilations of such records and other information upon request of the Commission." Though there can be no doubt that this prescription commits the members of the regime to a serious program of record keeping, the exact content of this obligation is not spelled out in the Convention, and it is important to bear in mind that the Commission can do little to clarify such obligations without the explicit consent of the Contracting Parties. Over and above the keeping of records, the Convention makes it clear that the Contracting Parties are expected to participate in good faith in the research activities organized by the Commission. In practice, this has come to mean support for and participation in the meetings of the standing committee on biology and research and its subcommittees.[18] Most of the actual work of this group is carried out in the various subcommittees, which include members from each of the Contracting Parties and which meet for approximately two weeks prior to the annual meeting of the Commission.

Finally, the INPFC includes a prescription obligating the Contracting Parties to take certain steps involving the formulation and implementation of domestic laws and regulations. Specifically, Article IX(2) states that "Each Contracting Party agrees, for purposes of rendering effective the

[17] Thus, Article III(1)(c)(ii) has the Commission deciding on and making recommendations concerning ". . . necessary joint conservation measures . . ."

[18] This committee is established under rule no. 12 of the INPFC Rules of Procedure. Its various subcommittees include one on salmon and others on Bering Sea groundfish, on groundfish of the Northeast Pacific, and on king and tanner crabs.

provisions of this Convention, to enact and enforce necessary laws and regulations, with regard to its nationals and fishing vessels, with appropriate penalties against violations thereof and to transmit to the Commission a report on any action taken by it with regard thereto." The general intent of this prescription is clear enough. Nevertheless, the prescription is quite inexact concerning the content of the obligations of the Contracting Parties. What sorts of laws and regulations are these parties expected to devise, and is there any way of reviewing their adequacy? Just what would constitute "appropriate penalties" for the kinds of violations likely to occur under these laws and regulations? How extensive an effort are the Contracting Parties obligated to make in tracking down suspected violators? Precisely what information are the Contracting Parties required to transmit to the Commission under the terms of Article IX(2)? Clear-cut answers to these questions do not exist. Therefore, it must be concluded that there is considerable room for disagreement concerning the level of compliance with this provision on the part of individual Contracting Parties.

How significant are these prescriptions? Do they seriously restrict the freedom of action of the Contracting Parties; do they require the parties to give up anything important or to accept real burdens? In the case of Japan, it is difficult to avoid concluding that the abstention rules constitute serious restrictions. It is true that Japan was not in a position to argue about the formulation of these rules in 1952 and that the provisional abstention line at 175° W has permitted Japanese fishermen to harvest some salmon of North American origin over the years. Nevertheless, the abstention rules have placed distinct limitations on the growth of certain Japanese high seas fishing operations in the North Pacific. As far as Canada and the United States are concerned, the prescriptions of the INPFC seem less restrictive but not unimportant. They do commit these parties to the acceptance of some Japanese fishing in the region. By implication at least, they place the burden of proof on Canada and the United States in demonstrating that the conditions for Japanese abstention spelled out in Article IV are being met on a continuous basis.[19] Canada and the United States also acknowledge serious responsibilities in the realm of conservation under the terms of the Convention. But it seems reasonable to conclude that these parties would have compelling reasons to formulate and carry out similar programs of conservation even if the INPFC did not exist. More generally, the Convention (if taken seriously) commits the Contracting Parties to make a good faith effort to move in the direction of coordinated management practices for the marine fisheries of the North Pacific. As I shall suggest later on, actual practice under the INPFC leaves much

[19] Article III(1)(a) gives the following directions to the Commission: "In regard to any stock of fish specified in the Annex, study for the purpose of determining annually whether such stock continues to qualify for abstention under the provisions of Article IV."

to be desired. Still, it would be a mistake to conclude that the prescriptions of the Convention are trivial or insignificant.

COMPLIANCE MECHANISMS

The problems of compliance associated with the INPFC differ substantially from those arising in conjunction with the Partial Test Ban Treaty. The actors actually engaging in fishing operations are relatively large numbers of private entities rather than a few public authorities. Moreover, the activities involved are ongoing and continuous over long periods of time; they are not confined to a small number of discrete and temporally specific acts.[20] To make matters more complex, detection of violations of some of the INPFC prescriptions is difficult, and chances of clandestine violations are not negligible. In all these respects, the prescriptions of the INPFC bear more resemblance to typical municipal or domestic prescriptions than to the major prescriptions of the Partial Test Ban Treaty.

It is noteworthy that this situation has not led to the emergence of a single, centralized public authority to deal with compliance problems. The Commission is weak and clearly not intended to play a major role in the realm of compliance. But the situation has induced the Contracting Parties to establish a clear-cut system of institutionalized arrangements to handle the compliance problems arising under the three-nation regime. What has emerged is a set of decentralized institutions.[21]

By far the most extensive provisions relating to compliance under this regime are those associated with the abstention rules described in the preceding section.[22] In general, the Contracting Parties agree ". . . to cooperate with each other in taking appropriate and effective measures . . ." to ensure compliance [Article X(1)]. But a series of more specific provisions follows this general formula. Article X(1)(a) addresses the issue of surveillance and provides for inspection of any suspected violator by officials of *any* Contracting Party. It states that ". . . the duly authorized officials of any Contracting Party may board such vessel to inspect its equipment, books, documents, and other articles and question the persons on board."[23] Accordingly, it is clear that the Contracting Parties possess the right to engage in extensive surveillance activities, though it is less clear whether they have a duty to do so as well.[24]

---

[20] By and large, the relevant activities do not take place on a year-round basis. They are concentrated heavily in the months of June, July, and August.

[21] For comparisons with other arrangements relating to marine fisheries consult Koers (1973).

[22] A more general study which is helpful in placing this discussion in perspective is Burke, Legatski, and Woodhead (1975).

[23] This provision has been construed broadly enough to permit authorized officials to inspect the contents of the holds of fishing vessels.

[24] This last point is important since some commentators have argued that the Japanese, in particular, have not been sufficiently energetic in tracking down violators of the abstention rules.

There are additional provisions pertaining to the apprehension of alleged violators. Article X(1)(b) states that the duly authorized official(s) of any Contracting Party may "arrest or seize" persons or vessels found engaging in violations of the Convention or suspected of having done so immediately prior to the actual inspection. In such cases, ". . . the Contracting Party to which the official belongs shall notify the Contracting Party to which such person or vessel belongs of such arrest or seizure, and shall deliver such vessel or persons as promptly as practicable to the authorized officials of the Contracting Party to which such vessel or person belongs at a place to be agreed upon by both Parties." The application of actual sanctions is then left to the authorities of the ". . . Party to which the above-mentioned person or fishing vessel belongs . . ." [Article X(1)(c)]. These authorities are entitled to proceed with the prosecution of offenders under the terms of their own municipal procedures, subject only to the stipulation concerning "appropriate penalties" included in Article IX. There is, however, a final provision calling for the transmission of ". . . witnesses and evidence necessary for establishing the offense . . ." to the ". . . Contracting Party having jurisdiction to try the offense . . ." [Article X(1)(c)].

The formal compliance mechanisms associated with the other prescriptions of the INPFC are more rudimentary. With respect to conservation measures, Article X(2) merely states that ". . . the Contracting Parties concerned shall carry out enforcement severally and jointly." This is undoubtedly meant to suggest the appropriateness of a highly decentralized set of institutions, though the Convention is largely silent concerning the content and character of these institutions. The one restriction it does introduce in this connection is an obligation on the part of those parties responsible for conservation ". . . to report periodically through the Commission to the Contracting Party which has agreed to abstain from the exploitation of such stocks of fish on the enforcement conditions, and also, if requested to provide opportunity for observation of the conduct of enforcement" [Article X(2)]. The contrast between these provisions and the arrangements associated with the abstention rules is striking.

No formal compliance mechanisms at all are associated with the prescription relating to information gathering and the conduct of research, but this omission is not a particularly serious one. Once a party becomes enmeshed in the whole system of procedures connected with the Commission and the standing committee on biology and research, it is difficult indeed to refuse to comply with periodic requests for information pertaining to harvests in the marine fisheries as well as conservation measures.[25] Of course, this in no way ensures quality control of the information transmitted to the Commission or introduced into the discussions of the subcommittees of the committee on biology and research. But even the most

---

[25] In fact, all three Contracting Parties have transmitted substantial volumes of information to the Commission on a regular basis.

elaborate compliance mechanisms could not guarantee quality control in this realm because it is difficult to distinguish between high and low quality information on marine fisheries. Finally, the Convention also omits formal compliance mechanisms in conjunction with the prescription relating to the development of domestic laws and regulations. As mentioned previously, the Contracting Parties are obligated to transmit information to the Commission concerning actions taken pursuant to these laws and regulations. Accordingly, a general failure to proceed vigorously in this area would be difficult to hide from public awareness over time. But the fact remains that there are no institutionalized arrangements designed to prod the Contracting Parties into complying with this prescription.[26]

In addition to institutionalized arrangements, several informal or *de facto* compliance mechanisms play some role in the calculations concerning compliance of the members of the INPFC. For example, major violations by one Contracting Party may trigger unilateral actions by another member aimed at altering the operation of the regime to the disadvantage of the violator. The party with most to fear along these lines within the framework of the INPFC has always been Japan. Recent developments make it plain that such fears have been well founded.[27] Violators of the INPFC prescriptions must also reckon with the fact that retaliatory measures will typically be feasible either in the same functional area or in some other domain. To illustrate, the United States and Japan have the capacity to bring effective pressure to bear on each other not only with respect to numerous diplomatic-strategic issues (for example, security guarantees, military bases, landing rights) but also with respect to a wide range of economic matters (exports of finished goods to the United States, the supply of crude oil to Japan, trade in timber, and others). The fact that the members of the INPFC are all industrialized states and highly interdependent in many areas only heightens the relevance of this sort of informal compliance mechanism.[28] Beyond this, there are the broader political implications of serious breaches of agreements between or among allied states. The possibility of disturbing relations among allies may not prevent states from embarking on serious conflicts over matters pertaining to natural resources. The recent "cod wars" between Great Britain and Iceland make this clear. Nevertheless, there can be little doubt that prospects of this sort have some deterrent effect, at least with respect to blatant violations of major agreements.

[26] A final point concerning these compliance mechanisms is that Article X(3) of the Convention provides for the Contracting Parties ". . . to meet, during the sixth year of the operation of this Convention to review the effectiveness of the enforcement provisions of this article and, if desirable, to consider means by which they may more effectively be carried out." This arrangement did not, however, yield any alterations of the original provisions.

[27] The extensions of Canadian and American fisheries jurisdictions to 200 miles have been promulgated unilaterally.

[28] For a more general discussion of the mutual vulnerability associated with high levels of interdependence see Young (1969).

Informal compliance mechanisms of this sort will almost certainly figure more prominently in the calculations of governments than in those of individual fishermen or operators who will ordinarily be more concerned with the maximization of short-term economic gain.[29] Moreover, some of the phenomena described in the preceding paragraph (for example, retaliatory measures in other functional areas) will have no direct consequences at all for individual fishermen, though they may be of great concern to the relevant governments. Under the circumstances, these informal compliance mechanisms have obvious limitations as responses to the compliance problems of the INPFC. Nevertheless, it would be a serious mistake to dismiss them.

THE RECORD

It is not a simple matter to evaluate the record of compliance with the prescriptions of the North Pacific Fisheries Convention. Some of the prescriptions are difficult to formulate in operational terms so that it is not easy to determine just what would constitute violations. It is hard to ensure quality control with respect to data pertaining to marine fisheries, a fact that makes it possible for subjects to engage in subtle violations in some areas. There is no reason to assume that inspection capabilities will be adequate to detect all violations of the INPFC prescriptions. Accordingly, the possibility of clandestine violations must be taken seriously. Moreover, some of the provisions of the agreement provoke strong emotional responses, a condition that is not conducive to objective assessments concerning the extent to which violations are occurring. These problems are by no means trivial, and they should be kept in mind in the following evaluation of the compliance record.

Consider first the case of the abstention rules. At the outset, it is important to note that Japanese fishermen do not fish for herring in any area adjacent to the restricted zone. Nor do Canadians exhibit any serious interest in harvesting salmon of North American origin in the Bering Sea. This reduces our focus of attention to Japanese activities relating to salmon and halibut of North American origin. Next, it seems reasonable to distinguish among several types of violations: (1) major incursions, (2) minor hedging such as small-scale and unsystematic crossings of the abstention line at 175° W, and (3) marginal or technical violations such as the retention of a few incidental salmon or halibut for crew use. My view is that we should concern ourselves primarily with the incidence and consequences of major incursions. Minor hedging is common to most compliance systems; it is nothing to become unduly concerned about, at least from the point of view of the relevant ecosystems or the social system as a whole.[30]

---

[29] That is, they are apt to employ a high discount rate in computing the present significance of events that can be expected to occur in the future.

[30] Of course, there may be cases in which minor hedging of this sort is of some real importance to individual members of the social system.

By the same token, technical violations are ultimately a trivial matter. They have little or no bearing on the viability of behavioral prescriptions or on the chances of achieving the objectives underlying a compliance system.

It will also help to differentiate three types of situation involving violations of the abstention rules. To begin with, there are situations in which violators are detected, handed over to the party possessing jurisdiction, and ultimately convicted. Then, there are cases in which one of the Contracting Parties alleges the occurrence of violations and makes arrests but in which the state with jurisdiction ultimately dismisses the charges on the grounds of insufficient evidence. With respect to the abstention rules of the INPFC, such cases invariably involve American charges relating to alleged violations by Japanese fishermen.[31] Finally, there are violations that simply go undetected. These are breaches of the INPFC abstention rules that never come to the attention of the authorized officials of the Contracting Parties.

It is a straightforward matter to examine the first two of these types of situation. During the period 1961–76, the United States formally charged Japanese operators with violations of the terms of the INPFC on nineteen occasions (NMFS, Law Enforcement Division, 1976). There is no record of formal charges of this sort being made in the years prior to 1961.[32] Nor is there any record that Canada charged Japan with violations of the abstention rules. Of the nineteen cases, ten have led to convictions and the imposition of sanctions, four (those for 1976) were unsettled at the time of writing, and five were dismissed by the Japanese authorities on grounds of insufficient evidence.[33] The most common sanction in these cases was the suspension of the vessel(s) rights to catch fish for a specified number of days. The seriousness of these penalties depends upon calendar dates as well as the length of time involved. Other penalties included fines, forfeiture of sums equivalent to the value of the relevant catch, and suspended sentences for captains and fishing masters. Over all, this certainly does not amount to a record of wholesale violations of the INPFC abstention rules. Nor does the ratio of convictions to dismissals indicate that the Japanese authorities have attempted to make light of the rules. In fact, it is generally agreed that the Japanese have become more (rather than less) vigorous over the years in prosecuting alleged violators.

The difficult problem, of course, is to assess the incidence and significance of undetected violations of the abstention rules. In the nature of things,

---

[31] So far as I have been able to determine, Canada has not made any formal charges concerning Japanese violations of the INPFC abstention rules.

[32] This does not of course prove that no such charges were made during the years 1953–60.

[33] These conclusions are based on the memorandum of the National Marine Fisheries Service, cited above, together with information supplied by the International North Pacific Fisheries Commission.

it is impossible to obtain firm evidence concerning this matter; indirect hints and scraps of information are all that is available.[34] Moreover, this is an area where emotions are not only strong but also apt to color judgments extensively. Consequently, it is hardly surprising that there are wide differences of opinion concerning undetected violations of the abstention rules and that judgments about this matter correlate highly with the interests of the parties making them.[35] I cannot hope to offer any definitive conclusions concerning this question of undetected violations. Nevertheless, I have formulated certain composite judgments on the basis of my detailed enquiry into the record of the INPFC.

The probability that major and systematic violations of the INPFC abstention rules would go undetected for very long is exceedingly low. Such violations would require extensive physical operations; they would not be randomly distributed throughout the Convention area, and they would almost certainly show up in information gathered by aerial patrols.[36] For all practical purposes, then, it is possible to rule out the occurrence of large and continuing violations along these lines. On the other hand, there can be little doubt that some real amount of minor hedging occurs. It seems probable that such violations most often take the form of brief incursions across the abstention line at 175° W. It is widely believed that these violations commonly involve Japanese "land-based" salmon gill-netters, not high seas factory ship fleets.[37] The fact that the gillnetters do not operate in large fleets so that their movements are harder to follow lends credence to this view. There is no reason to suspect that the Japanese government is in any way encouraging violations of this type. On the contrary, the Japanese authorities have apparently become more vigorous in prosecuting and penalizing violators of the INPFC abstention rules in recent years. This is not to suggest that these violations are either uncommon or unimportant, but it does indicate that the problem is primarily one of controlling the fishermen and operators rather than altering the attitude of the Japanese government.

Before leaving the subject of the abstention rules, it seems relevant to say something about the incidental catch of halibut in Japanese trawling

[34] For example, the capture of salmon with previous gill net markings is an indicator of possible violations of the abstention rule pertaining to salmon.

[35] For an argument suggesting that violations are widespread see Oliver (1968). On the other hand, several of those with whom I talked in preparing this study take the opposite point of view.

[36] The United States Coast Guard, for example, currently employs approximately 1,600 hours of C-130 time and 600 hours of H-3 helicopter time per year in mounting aerial patrols in the Convention area. While these patrols are not devoted exclusively to INPFC concerns, the chances of major incursions going undetected under these conditions are slim.

[37] These land-based gillnetters operate far from their home bases. But they are more prevalent in the southern portions of the Convention area than in its northern portions.

operations. The facts are simple (Hoag and French, 1976). Japanese trawling operations in the Convention area bring up substantial numbers of
halibut as an incidental catch. Some of these halibut are taken in the abstention zone demarcated in the INPFC Annex as amended. There is no
way to eliminate this incidental catch altogether without terminating trawling operations aimed at the harvest of other groundfish. Incidental catches
of this type have not been construed as violations of the INPFC abstention
rule so long as a good-faith effort is made to return the halibut to the sea.
But this practice is a controversial one. Those who object to it point out
that the mortality rate among halibut returned to the sea in this fashion
is extremely high, resulting in a waste of animal protein for human con-
sumption (Wilimovsky, 1976). The defenders of the practice claim that a
policy of allowing fishermen to retain incidental catches of halibut would
encourage operators to initiate various unacceptable practices aimed at
increasing the magnitude of these catches on a *de facto* basis.

In summary, the situation relating to violations of the abstention rules is
relatively complex. Nevertheless, it is hard to avoid the conclusion that
compliance with the formal requirements of the abstention rules has been
quite good. At least this is so by comparison with the record of the typical
municipal or domestic prescription. There have obviously been violations
of these rules, but they have hardly been extensive enough to bring the
viability of the whole system into question. And there is no evidence to
warrant the conclusion that the Japanese government has encouraged such
violations.

Turning to the issue of compliance with the prescription concerning conservation measures, it seems helpful to draw several initial distinctions.
This prescription applies only to the Contracting Parties, but in recent
years, the high seas fishing operations of several noncontracting parties in
the Convention area have grown to major proportions. Therefore, compliance with this prescription by the Contracting Parties is now clearly
insufficient to guarantee the protection of the relevant stocks of marine fish
(Hoag and French, 1976). Beyond this, the INPFC does not establish any
specific compliance requirements for species other than those referred to
explicitly in the Annex. For example, it offers no real protection for stocks
of various groundfish (other than halibut) which have been seriously
depleted during the last ten to fifteen years.[38] There is of course no formal
barrier to the formulation of additional conservation measures within the
framework of the INPFC regime. In practice, however, it has proven exceedingly difficult to reach agreement among the three national sections of
the INPFC Commission on the formulation of such measures. Even in the
odd case where the Commission has been able to reach consensus on a
recommendation (for example, halibut setline fishing in the eastern Bering

[38] Prominent examples include pollock, Pacific Ocean perch, hake, and blackcod or
sablefish.

Sea), the measure has not been accepted by the governments of the Contracting Parties.

With respect to the species listed in the INPFC Annex, the case of halibut is worthy of separate attention. Here the United States and Canada have developed and carried out an extensive program of joint conservation measures within the framework of the International Pacific Halibut Convention (Skud, 1976). There is general agreement that these measures were relatively successful prior to the emergence of large-scale Japanese and Soviet trawling operations in the eastern Bering Sea and the Gulf of Alaska. Unfortunately, these operations, aimed at other species of groundfish, have brought up substantial quantities of halibut as an incidental catch, and have done considerable damage to the halibut stocks of the Convention area, particularly in the eastern Bering Sea. As noted previously, these operations, even in the case of Japan, do not involve formal violations of any prescription of the INPFC.

In the cases of salmon and herring, Canada and the United States pursue largely independent conservation programs.[39] Canadian efforts are predominantly under the jurisdiction of the federal government, primary responsibility lying with the Department of the Environment and the Department of National Defense. There are apparently continuing problems of coordination between these agencies in the administration of conservation measures. But it is clear that the Canadian government's concern about the conservation of stocks of salmon and herring has grown rapidly in recent years.

The situation in the United States differs considerably due to the complex separation of authority over such matters between the federal government and the state governments.[40] With respect to the Convention area, the key role in the development of conservation measures for salmon and herring has been played (since 1959) by the government of the state of Alaska.[41] But the federal government has never been entirely uninvolved in this realm (for example, it has promulgated regulations for high seas salmon net fishing), and the federal role is growing as a consequence of the passage of the Fishery Conservation and Management Act of 1976.[42] Within Alaska's government, responsibility for the development of con-

[39] A prominent exception is the system of conservation measures associated with the Fraser River salmon agreement.

[40] Under the terms of the Submerged Lands Act of 1953 (PL 83-31) the states have jurisdiction over fisheries out to the three-mile limit of territorial waters. Whether the impending extension of territorial waters to twelve miles will lead to a corresponding extension of state jurisdiction remains to be seen.

[41] Prior to 1958, Alaska was a territory administered by the federal government rather than a state in its own right. This status changed under the terms of the Alaska Statehood Act of 1958 (PL 85-508).

[42] Preliminary experience with the regional fisheries councils (the North Pacific Fisheries Council in the case of the Convention area) suggests that they are likely to play an active role in the development of conservation measures.

servation measures lies with the Department of Fish and Game. This Department operates an elaborate system of regulations for salmon of North American origin (the regulations for herring are considerably less extensive).[43] Whether or not this system of regulations is ideal, there can be no doubt that it reflects a serious concern for the conservation of the relevant stocks. Recently, responsibility for the enforcement of these regulations has been transferred to the Alaska Department of Public Safety. There are indications that this shift will lead to a more vigorous approach to the problem of enforcement.

Though the conservation prescription of the INPFC applies primarily to Canada and the United States, it has some bearing on the behavior of Japanese fishermen as well. This is so both because the location of the abstention line at 175° W has allowed the Japanese to develop a high seas fishery for salmon in the Convention area and because of the incidental catch problem affecting halibut. It is fashionable in certain North American circles to portray the Japanese as being unconcerned with conservation problems in these realms, but this view does not accord fully with the evidence. The Japanese government has promulgated a number of domestic regulations pertaining to the harvest of salmon on the high seas and it has cooperated in the development of certain conservation measures for halibut, particularly in the eastern Bering Sea where the problem appears to be most severe.[44] Whether these measures are adequate and vigorously enforced is another matter. But it is clearly not appropriate to paint a simplistic picture according to which scrupulous Canadian and American efforts to fulfill the conservation prescription of the INPFC are being frustrated solely by a total lack of concern for the conservation problem on the part of the Japanese.

Does the existence of all these conservation measures permit us to conclude that the level of compliance with the conservation prescription of the INPFC has generally been high? Unfortunately, the fact that the prescription itself is not operational makes it impossible to formulate any decisive answer to this question. There can be no doubt that the principal subjects of this prescription, Canada and the United States, have developed extensive conservation programs relating to the stocks in question. Moreover, it seems clear that concern about conservation problems in the Convention area has grown rapidly in recent years. Whether the resultant programs are adequate for the achievement of their basic goals, however, is much more doubtful. This is partly because many aspects of the conservation problem with respect to marine fisheries are poorly understood (Larkin, 1977). In part, it is because the INPFC regime has no force with

[43] Apparently, much less is known about the population dynamics of herring than of salmon, so that it is difficult to formulate effective conservation measures for herring.

[44] The Japan Fisheries Agency (JFA) also takes an active interest in efforts to obtain compliance with these regulations.

respect to the behavior of noncontracting parties, and also because the incidental catch problem has not been fully resolved within the framework of the Convention's prescriptions. The crucial problems, therefore, seem endemic to the INPFC regime itself; they are not a consequence of violations of the conservation prescription as it is written.

Consider now the INPFC prescription concerning information gathering and research. Again, there is no operational standard to determine what would constitute full compliance with this prescription. Consequently, it is not surprising that judgments differ markedly concerning the record associated with the prescription. One view holds that this prescription, especially in its Article VIII formulation, has been complied with fully by the Contracting Parties. Members of the Commission's secretariat, for example, argue that they have encountered no serious problems in obtaining relevant information from the three Contracting Parties. There is also some objective support for this argument. An examination of the series of annual reports prepared by the Commission makes it clear that the parties have transmitted a great deal of information in purely quantitative terms. Further, discussions with participants confirm that the national sections have participated vigorously in the deliberations within the subcommittees of the biology and research committee.[45]

An alternative view, however, suggests that the Contracting Parties have treated this prescription cavalierly even though they have not violated it openly. The argument here is that "subtle" violations are both feasible and common in this context. Partly, this is due to data problems. The absence of consensus on standard indicators and measures relating to marine fisheries not only introduces a serious note of ambiguity, it also makes it nearly impossible to ensure quality control with respect to the data transmitted to the Commission. For example, there is little doubt that selective reporting with respect to INPFC matters has occurred from time to time, and it is probable that some cases of conscious distortion have occurred as well. Other "subtle" violations have arisen from the extensive politicization of the biology and research committee. Though this committee is meant to be an objective or scientific body, political pressures have played a prominent part in the deliberations of its subcommittees. Thus, individual participants have been heavily influenced by the heads of their respective delegations, and many of the discussions have failed to conform to the standards of scientific debate. The relatively imprecise character of fisheries biology has no doubt facilitated the introduction of subjective or political considerations into these discussions. Nevertheless, this problem is of undeniable importance, and it raises real questions concerning the extent

[45] Each of the Contracting Parties also conducts extensive research in preparation for these meetings: the Japanese at the Far Seas Fisheries Research Laboratory in Shimizu, the Canadians at the Pacific Biological Station in Nanaimo, and the Americans at the Northwest and Alaska Fisheries Center in Seattle.

to which the Contracting Parties have lived up to their research commitments.[46]

Finally, there is the question of the extent to which the Contracting Parties have complied with the prescription concerning domestic laws and regulations set forth in Article IX(2) of the Convention. Each of the parties has enacted extensive sets of laws and regulations applicable to INPFC matters. For the most part, there is general agreement that these laws and regulations are adequate, in principle, to render effective the provisions of the INPFC. The real question is the extent to which they are vigorously enforced. Here too, the absence of an operational standard makes it difficult to reach definitive conclusions. Nevertheless, some comments concerning this issue are in order.

The record of Japan is relatively good and generally thought to be improving when violations are brought explicitly to the attention of the government. Penalties in the forms of suspensions, forfeitures, and fines have assumed serious proportions, and the government has exhibited growing vigor in the prosecution of violators. The principal controversy concerns the extent to which the Japanese government does enough to prevent violations or apprehend violators before the United States or Canada brings violations to its attention.[47] In fact, the current posture of Japan on this issue does not seem unreasonable. The incidence of major violations of the relevant laws and regulations is evidently not extreme. Japan has an unusually extensive set of high seas fisheries to attend to and cannot be expected to devote all its attention to the Convention area of the INPFC. And it seems reasonable for Canada and the United States to assume primary responsibility for such surveillance since these parties are also the principal beneficiaries of the INPFC abstention system.

The relevant domestic laws of Canada and the United States pertain to conservation measures rather than abstention rules. In both cases, there is currently a good deal of ambiguity and uncertainty concerning the enforcement of applicable laws and regulations. As far as Canada is concerned, this appears to stem from the fragmentation of responsibility among several agencies of the federal government (Middlemiss, 1976). In the United States, there is the added complication of achieving coordination between the federal government and the state of Alaska. It would, however, be difficult to demonstrate that either Canada or the United States has failed in any fundamental way to fulfill its obligations under Article IX(2) of the INPFC. Furthermore, both parties are now taking definite steps to improve their performance in this area. The movement

[46] Among other things, this case illustrates the problems facing scientists in their efforts to make constructive contributions to the formulation of public policy.

[47] Specifically, the question is whether the Japan Fisheries Agency should augment its activities relating to surveillance and the apprehension of violators in the Convention area.

toward coordination between the Department of the Environment and the Department of National Defense within the Canadian government is important in this connection. Similarly, both the shift of enforcement responsibilities to the Department of Public Safety within the Alaskan state government and the growing coordination between the Coast Guard and the National Marine Fisheries Service at the federal level suggest parallel developments in the American case.[48]

In summary, compliance with the formal requirements of the INPFC prescriptions is relatively high on the part of all the Contracting Parties. A comparison with any typical municipal or domestic compliance system is not likely to be unfavorable to the INPFC prescriptions. Nevertheless, some commentators argue that the spirit of the Convention has been violated in important ways, even in the absence of formal violations. For example, the Japanese harvest of salmon of North American origin west of 175° W is regarded by some as a violation of the spirit of the INPFC (Emberg, 1977). In fact, the matter is not clear-cut. Much depends on interpretations of the original intentions underlying the Convention, assessments of the condition of the relevant stocks, and evaluations of elusive data concerning the actual magnitude of the Japanese harvest. Next, the politicization of the committee on biology and research is sometimes pointed to as a serious violation of the spirit of the Convention. There can be no doubt that this is a significant problem. Nevertheless, it is worth noting that problems of this sort arise in connection with many compliance systems (municipal as well as international) and that the problem is no more severe in the case at hand than it is in numerous other systems, the usefulness of which is seldom questioned. Finally, the obviously self-interested character of the debates relating to the application of the conditions of Article IV and the failure of the procedures for adjusting the INPFC abstention rules can be taken as evidence of an unwillingness on the part of the Contracting Parties to conform to the spirit of the INPFC. To the extent that this suggests that the INPFC regime has proven incapable of coping effectively with changes in the fundamental character of the marine fisheries of the North Pacific it is undoubtedly valid. Even so, it should not be allowed to obscure the fact that the Contracting Parties have generally complied with the specific prescriptions of the Convention.

The crucial problems of the INPFC regime stem from the failure to employ economic reasoning in managing the relevant stocks, the growing importance of high seas fishing by noncontracting parties, the difficulties associated with the management of stocks not referred to explicitly in the Annex, and the inability of the Commission to find ways of solving complex issues (such as the incidental catch problem in the case of halibut). These problems are clearly of fundamental importance, and they obviously

[48] Administrative responsibility for enforcement measures relating to the Convention area is now concentrated effectively in the Juneau offices of the relevant agencies.

underlie the current move to shunt the INPFC regime aside in favor of arrangements based on coastal state jurisdiction. Nevertheless, most of these problems can hardly be blamed on the Convention itself, and nothing in this argument alters the fact that the Contracting Parties have compiled a relatively good record of compliance with the explicit requirements of the INPFC prescriptions.

ANALYSIS

The record of compliance with the explicit prescriptions of the INPFC is not as striking as the record compiled under the Partial Nuclear Test Ban, but the level of compliance has clearly been sufficient to maintain the viability of these prescriptions. It compares favorably with the record associated with any typical municipal or domestic prescription. And, compliance with the major prescriptions has improved during recent years. How are we to account for these results, given the fact that the INPFC regime does not include a highly developed or centralized public authority?

In thinking about this question, it is important to draw a distinction between the two levels of actors involved in the compliance problems of the INPFC: fishermen or fishing operators and the governments of the Contracting Parties. Though it is hazardous to generalize too facilely, it does seem feasible to characterize the typical fishing interests as economically marginal and operating with extremely short time horizons. This is partly attributable to the intrinsic difficulties of common property arrangements (Gordon, 1954). But it also stems from a variety of more specific inefficiencies in the organization of the fishing industry, at least in the United States and Canada. Under the circumstances, it is to be expected that fishermen will tend to fish whenever and wherever they can get away with it. This tendency is no doubt reinforced by the mystique of rugged independence common among fishermen, a mental set that produces a lack of receptivity toward the efforts of regulatory agencies to manage marine fisheries. All this suggests that compliance with prescriptions relating to marine fisheries will require some real enforcement system when it comes to the activities of the fishermen themselves (Christy and Scott, 1965).

The principal burden of obtaining compliance with the prescriptions of the INPFC, therefore, falls on the governments of the Contracting Parties. Why have these governments generally favored such compliance and even taken relatively vigorous steps to obtain it? Consider first the case of Japan. Compliance with the abstention rules has always been conceptualized as a *quid pro quo* for continued access to the high-seas fisheries of the Convention area. In the aggregate, these fisheries are of great importance to the Japanese, and there is always the possibility of unilateral actions on the part of Canada or the United States which would impose severe restrictions on Japanese freedom of entry. A Japanese policy of complying carefully with the prescriptions of the INPFC has the virtue, therefore, of avoiding any provocation for unilateral actions by the other two parties, though of course it constitutes no guarantee against the occurrence of such actions.[49] Beyond this, it seems clear that the Japanese government (in contrast to the fishing interests) is significantly affected by a concern for the long-term viability of the relevant fisheries. It is fashionable in some circles to criticize the Japanese for a willingness to exhaust marine fisheries in a somewhat reckless fashion, but the evidence does not suggest that they are oblivious to the long-term problems of conserving the stocks of the North Pacific. Japanese research on marine fisheries is extensive and sophisticated, and the heavy dependence of Japan on fish as a source of animal protein gives the government a well-developed interest in the continued viability of the fisheries of the Convention area. Though it would undoubtedly be easy to overemphasize incentives of this type, there is reason to believe that they have become increasingly influential in Japan in recent years.

For the Canadian and American governments, the central issue concerns compliance with conservation measures rather than abstention rules. Here several factors seem relevant. Mounting evidence of long-term declines in the harvests of certain species, such as salmon of North American origin, has begun to have a serious impact on the thinking of public officials.[50] Further, it now seems clear that potential harvests from marine fisheries are subject to relatively severe constraints, a fact that emphasizes the importance of taking vigorous steps to maintain the viability of existing fisheries.[51] Relatively powerful interest groups have also demonstrated an ability to bring effective pressure to bear on the governments of Canada and the United States to carry out serious conservation programs in the Convention area. This is especially true in cases where these conservation programs involve efforts to reduce foreign access to the fisheries and to reserve the stocks for Canadian or American fishermen. More recently, however, the environmental movement has succeeded in inducing both these governments to place a higher priority on the conservation of renewable resources as an important policy objective in its own right. Under the circumstances, the coalition supporting genuine conservation measures in the Convention area is now a formidable one which can expect to have its views taken seriously.

It is also interesting to contemplate the costs of obtaining compliance with the INPFC prescriptions. How much do various public authorities invest in efforts to achieve compliance with these prescriptions and are they

[49] The recent unilateral actions of Canada and the United States in extending their fisheries jurisdiction to 200 miles make this abundantly clear.

[50] For relevant time-series data see Buck (1973).

[51] The magnitude of potential harvests from marine fisheries is a much debated subject. For background information see Gulland (1972).

getting good value from their investments? Not surprisingly, it is difficult to answer this question. Above all, there are serious problems of computation. The governments of the Contracting Parties do not keep records that make it possible to single out expenditures relating to INPFC prescriptions. The costs are borne not only by several governments but also by various agencies within these governments. Therefore, it is necessary to deal with severe problems of aggregation in assessing investments aimed at the achievement of compliance. Beyond this, it is not self-evident what expenses to include in making these calculations. For example, it is hard to know how to treat fixed costs, in contrast to operating expenses. Although estimates of compliance costs must therefore be of the rough-and-ready variety, I believe it is possible to arrive at figures that are of the right order of magnitude.

In the American case, the Coast Guard has assumed primary responsibility for compliance with the INPFC prescriptions. Operating expenses for the Coast Guard in this realm may run as high as $1 million a year.[52] Much smaller sums are expended by the National Marine Fisheries Service —$250,000 a year is probably a liberal estimate. In addition, the Department of Public Safety of the Alaskan state government mounts an enforcement operation that is distinctly relevant to the conservation provisions of the INPFC.[53] This operation is certainly far smaller than that of the Coast Guard mentioned above; it is hard to see how it could run to more than $500,000 a year.

While the Canadian government takes a definite interest in the issue of compliance with INPFC prescriptions, there can be little doubt that the United States has borne the principal burden. So far as I can tell, Canadian expenses relate primarily to conservation measures and probably do not run over $500,000 a year. The case of Japan is a little different. Japanese expenses for compliance with INPFC prescriptions are of two types. First, there are the costs of prosecuting and penalizing violators brought to the attention of the Japanese government by the United States or Canada. As the number of cases of this type is small, these costs cannot be extreme. In addition, the Japan Fisheries Agency operates patrol boats that play some role in deterring and reacting to violations of the INPFC abstention

---

[52] The United States Coast Guard (17th District) currently makes use of some 1,100 vessel patrol days per year in carrying out its responsibilities relating to marine fisheries. The average cost per day is about $4,000 so that the total annual cost is $4,400,000. Of this sum, approximately one-tenth or $440,000 is attributed to INPFC-related matters. Parallel figures for aircraft (C-130 transports and H-3 helicopters) are 2,200 hours at about $1,100 per hour for a total of $2,200,000 per year. Again, about one-tenth of this involves INPFC-related matters so that this adds another $220,000 to operating expenses. In using the figure of $1 million a year, I have added an extra $340,000 to reflect the cost of administration, support personnel in Kodiak or Juneau, and so forth.

[53] Conversations with Alaskan fishermen suggest that this patrol system has become an extensive and effective operation in recent years.

rules.[54] It is difficult to estimate the cost of this operation, but it is undoubtedly smaller than the American Coast Guard operation referred to above. Therefore, it seems unlikely that total Japanese operating expenses attributable to the compliance problems of the INPFC run over $1 million a year.

This gives us a total of $3,250,000 as an estimate of annual operating expenses for all parties in the effort to obtain compliance with the INPFC prescriptions. Though it is hard to be certain, I would judge this to be a liberal estimate. To complete the picture, it is necessary to add some figure to reflect fixed costs, that is, the cost of equipment and facilities whose value depreciates over time. Government agencies frequently do not approach accounting in these terms, however, and there are numerous problems in determining the real costs of equipment and facilities.[55] Thus, it is infeasible to make anything but a rough estimate of fixed costs. Let us assume that fixed costs (computed on an annual basis) are similar in magnitude to total operating costs, or something like $3,250,000.[56] Again, I would regard this as a liberal estimate. Adding these figures gives us an estimate of $6,500,000 as the total annual investment on the part of all public authorities in efforts to obtain compliance with the prescriptions of the INPFC.

Is an annual investment of this magnitude rational for the parties concerned? Let us begin with a normative assessment. The first point to notice concerns the shapes of the relevant cost curves. There can be no doubt that increasing marginal compliance costs will obtain in this case. In fact, the marginal costs of obtaining compliance with the prescriptions of the INPFC can be expected to go up rapidly as the level of violations enters its lower reaches. It also seems reasonable to assume the occurrence of increasing marginal social costs. The INPFC regime would undoubtedly collapse if the level of violations of its prescriptions became too high.[57] All this implies that it is not rational to try and eliminate violations of INPFC prescriptions, though it is rational to make some real effort to control them.[58] This general expectation accords well with actual experience. Beyond this, it is difficult to reach precise conclusions. The present pro-

[54] Evidently, these patrols are more effective in the case of the high seas factory fleets operating in Area A than in the case of the "land-based" gillnetters operating in Area B.

[55] It is also difficult to determine what proportion of the cost of a given facility (for example, the Kodiak Support Center of the Coast Guard) is attributable to the enforcement of fisheries regulations in contrast to other functions, such as weather mapping and search and rescue missions.

[56] I am assuming here that it is reasonable to amortize fixed costs for accounting purposes over the lives of the relevant facilities.

[57] The introduction of intangible values (for example, the preservation of the natural environment of the Convention area) would only serve to reinforce this argument.

[58] The investment decisions of public authorities relating to compliance are analyzed in depth in chapter 7 infra.

gram of keeping overt violations down to a relatively low level (while largely ignoring "subtle" violations) is probably about right in normative terms. This conclusion reflects a presumption that marginal social costs rise more rapidly than marginal compliance costs over the relevant range. Surely, it would be hard to make a normative case for any large increase in expenditures on the achievement of compliance with the INPFC prescriptions. Increasing marginal compliance costs would constitute an effective barrier to any move of this sort.

Turning from normative propositions to empirical arguments, are any of the relevant public authorities likely to experience powerful incentives to depart from the normative equilibrium in the case of the INPFC? The principal incentive I can see to overinvest in the pursuit of compliance would stem from pressures exerted by certain special interest groups. It is reasonable to think of American or Canadian fishermen pressing for the enforcement of rules pertaining to Japanese high seas fishing,[59] and the environmental movement may well be a force to be reckoned with, at least in Canada and the United States. In my judgment, however, incentives for public authorities to underinvest are likely to be at least as strong in this case as incentives to overinvest. In part, this is attributable to the fact that the maintenance of the INPFC regime is a collective good, so that free-rider incentives are present. Yet this phenomenon may be offset to some extent by the fact that at least Canada and the United States are primarily interested in the viability of the stocks of fish in certain limited areas rather than in the Convention area as a whole.[60] Of greater importance, I expect, are the facts that the impact of many violations of INPFC prescriptions is only likely to be felt over the long run, and that the consequences of such violations are often difficult to pin down with any precision. Under the circumstances, public authorities may well feel that they can afford to take a somewhat relaxed view of violations without jeopardizing the security of their own positions. In the final analysis, it strikes me as unlikely that the balance of all these forces will induce public authorities to depart drastically from the posture suggested by the normative analysis of investments in the achievement of compliance with INPFC prescriptions. In any case, the actual behavior of the public authorities has been compatible with this expectation over the years 1953–77.

CONCLUSION

What are the broader implications of this case? Above all, an examination of the case does *not* lead to pessimistic conclusions about the pros-

---

[59] See Emberg (1977) for an illustration of the efforts of fishing interests to bring such pressure to bear.

[60] The fact that these parties can, at least to a degree, set up exclusion mechanisms in these domains will reduce their propensity to look upon the maintenance of the viability of the relevant stocks as a collective good.

pects of achieving relatively high levels of compliance in the international system or in other highly decentralized sociopolitical systems. It is true that violations of the INPFC prescriptions have occurred, but the level of violations has not been unusually high, at least by comparison with typical municipal or domestic prescriptions. Violations of the specific prescriptions of the Convention have certainly not undermined the viability of the INPFC regime. And, as one might expect, the level of compliance has generally been higher with the more explicit prescriptions, such as the abstention rules, than with the more intangible and nonoperational prescriptions, such as the prescription concerning coordinated research.

This suggests that decentralized systems of compliance mechanisms may be workable in specific, real-world situations. It seems evident that attempts to obtain compliance without organization (as in the case of the test ban) would not prove workable in this case, because of the central role of numerous private entities and the problems of detecting many types of violations. Nevertheless, there is nothing in the record of the INPFC to lead to the conclusion that a centralized public authority with substantial enforcement capabilities is necessary to achieve high levels of compliance with prescriptions of this sort. This strikes me as a finding of considerable importance for analyses of compliance in the international system (as well as in many other decentralized sociopolitical systems) since there are compelling reasons to conclude that substantially more centralized compliance arrangements will seldom be feasible politically at this level during the foreseeable future.

At the same time, it would be inappropriate to become unduly optimistic on the basis of this case study. It seems apparent that the INPFC regime is now collapsing under the weight of several differentiable factors. These include the insensitivity of the regime to the economics of marine fisheries, the problems arising from the expanding operations of noncontracting parties, the difficulties of regulating the exploitation of species not referred to explicitly in the INPFC Annex, and the more general trend toward the extension of coastal state jurisdiction over marine fisheries. None of this detracts from the fact that decentralized compliance mechanisms have achieved relatively high levels of compliance, but it does emphasize the fact that compliance systems, as well as regimes more generally, do not always yield fully satisfactory outcomes, and sometimes succumb to the forces of broader events even when they have been reasonably successful in terms of the compliance criterion.

PART III

Toward a more general theory of compliance

CHAPTER 6

The problem of
compliance reconsidered

Behavioral prescriptions are ubiquitous in the realm of human affairs. Even an isolated individual—a Robinson Crusoe—is almost certain to develop rules for himself; following certain rules will improve his chances of surviving and of enjoying a reasonably pleasant existence. In social systems, behavioral prescriptions typically emerge to regulate problems stemming from the interactions of individual actors. Even in relatively primitive societies, individuals will be dependent upon each other for some necessities of life, and the self-interested activities of individuals will frequently impinge upon the welfare or happiness of others. The standard method of managing the resultant problems is to introduce behavioral prescriptions in the form of rules, laws, moral precepts, and social norms. As a society becomes more highly developed, both the extensiveness and the importance of its behavioral prescriptions will increase markedly.[1] This is so because the level of interdependence among the members of a social system and the unintended effects of their actions on others rise rapidly as a function of development.

The purpose of this chapter is to lay a foundation for a more general theory of compliance. Specifically, I want to introduce some new concepts and to fill in some conceptual gaps in the initial formulation of the problem in this essay. The argument of the chapter is less fully developed in analytic terms than the material presented in the chapters of Part I. In essence, it constitutes an agenda for further research rather than a review of what has been done so far.

---

[1] Though I do not wish to propose a formal definition of development, I am concerned with phenomena like industrialization and urbanization in this connection.

BEHAVIORAL PRESCRIPTIONS

The concept "behavioral prescription" is a wide-ranging one which cuts across the boundaries of any standard discipline or field of study. A few examples will indicate the extent of this conceptual category. To begin with, some behavioral prescriptions take the form of rules or agreements not possessing the force or status of laws. The rules of grammar as well as the rules governing most games illustrate this type of prescription.[2] Next, laws, contracts, and treaties frequently embody behavioral prescriptions. These are prescriptions possessing formal legal status such as tax laws, speed limits, and zoning ordinances. It is worth noting, however, that not all laws properly belong to the category of behavioral prescriptions.[3] For example, some laws confer powers to perform specified actions and are not meant to serve as guides to conduct at all. Beyond this, there are numerous moral and ethical standards that demand compliance from various subject groups. Prescriptions requiring individuals to refrain from taking human life and to fulfill promises almost always exhibit this form. Finally, social norms often acquire prescriptive force and take on the characteristics of behavioral prescriptions among large groups of subjects. Specific standards of etiquette and "in-group" behavior take this form in many social systems.

Though these varieties of behavioral prescriptions are analytically differentiable, they need not be mutually exclusive. In fact, they commonly intersect with each other in complex ways. A particular prescription may be overdetermined in the sense that it rests on more than one of the bases referred to in the preceding paragraph. The prescription against the taking of human life, for example, is both a moral precept and a legal standard in most societies. Similarly, behavioral prescriptions may evolve over time from one form to another. Thus, there are numerous cases of standards that originated as moral precepts but that have gradually been incorporated into legal statutes with the passage of time. At the same time, it is not uncommon for behavioral prescriptions resting upon different sources of authority to conflict with one another. A classic illustration involves the soldier who receives a command from a superior to perform acts that clearly violate important moral standards.[4] But situations of this generic type occur in many walks of life. Individuals finding themselves in such situations will typically experience severe cross-pressures with respect to the problem of compliance, and the actual behavior that emerges under such conditions is well worth studying in some detail.

[2] See also the related conception of "conventions" in Lewis (1969).

[3] On this point, see the observations of Hart (1961, chaps. II and III). The same point is addressed from a different perspective by Dworkin (1967).

[4] The conflict here is not between the relevant moral standard and the specific command received. Rather it is a conflict between the moral standard and another behavioral prescription to the effect that subordinates in military organizations should obey the commands of their superiors.

Operationality and publicity

There are substantial differences among behavioral prescriptions in the extent to which they pose problems of operationality. Some prescriptions are formulated in such a way that their requirements are operational from the outset. There is little doubt about the operational content of a law to the effect that the speed limit on a certain highway is 55 mph at all times. Nor is there any ambiguity about the operational significance of a rule stating that the lights in a hospital ward are to be turned out at 9 pm. On the other hand, many behavioral prescriptions are not formulated in an intrinsically operational fashion, and problems of spelling out their operational content are sometimes severe.[5] For example, what is the precise operational content of a law prohibiting sex discrimination in the realm of employment? What is the exact coverage of a moral prohibition against lying in interpersonal relationships? What exactly is required under the terms of a rule requiring fair play in competitive sports? In all these cases, there are apt to be frequent disputes concerning the extent to which specific actions do or do not constitute violations of the prescriptions. As an empirical generalization, I would argue that problems of this type are common with respect to a high proportion of the most important behavioral prescriptions.

Efforts to cope with such problems often fail to tap the underlying problems at stake. Thus, it is possible to put laws against racial or sex discrimination into operation by introducing formal quotas or systems of preferential treatment, but such procedures do nothing to guarantee that the underlying biases or prejudices will disappear. Similarly, one can ban certain specified forms of overt collusion by making laws concerning the maintenance of economic competition, but this in no way eliminates the possibility of informal coordination designed to place restraints on competition. Nevertheless, if efforts to put such prescriptions into operation are abandoned, the whole issue of compliance becomes moot; it becomes impossible to reach unambiguous decisions concerning the extent to which the behavior of individual subjects conforms to the prescriptions in question. I do not believe there is any definitive solution to this dilemma.[6] It will always be necessary to approach it on a case-by-case basis, without expecting to arrive at a perfect solution in any given case.

It is also important to distinguish between operationality and publicity with respect to behavioral prescriptions. While operationality refers to the extent to which the actions required by a prescription are formulated precisely and in an empirically meaningful fashion, publicity refers to the com-

[5] Even when individual prescriptions are unambiguous, problems of operationality arise when individual prescriptions conflict with each other. The resultant problems are discussed in more detail later on in this section under the heading of "compliance systems."

[6] The existence of this problem is an important source of the role of judicial procedures in most social systems.

munication of requirements associated with prescriptions to the relevant subject groups. It seems clear that publicity is a necessary condition for the achievement of compliance. Subjects cannot be expected to act in accordance with a prescription unless they are informed about the actions it requires and the conditions under which these actions are appropriate.[7] Therefore, there will always be a *prima facie* case in favor of efforts aimed at publicizing currently accepted behavioral prescriptions.

However, there are several complications associated with the issue of publicity. First, some prescriptions are easier to publicize effectively than others. For example, it is less difficult to communicate the idea of simple quotas in connection with sex discrimination than to communicate elaborate schemes involving systems of preferential treatment. Second, publicity is not a free good from the point of view of public authorities. They will always be on the lookout for ways of cutting their costs by reducing expenditures on publicity. One technique that is commonly resorted to in order to reduce such expenditures is to shift the burden of knowledge onto the members of the subject groups. Thus, it is possible to assert that subjects are expected to inform themselves about behavioral prescriptions and that no distinctions will be made between violations attributable to ignorance and violations stemming from intentional actions.[8] This policy is summed up in the assertion that "ignorance of the law is no excuse." Third, there will be some situations in which public authorities deliberately refrain from unambiguous publicizing of requirements. This posture is sometimes used as a technique of control by authoritarian regimes. So long as the requirements of a prescription are not well publicized, there will be uncertainty in the minds of the subjects and the regime can apply the prescription selectively when it wishes to control the behavior of particular individuals.

Compliance systems

So far, I have been talking about behavioral prescriptions as though each one could be treated as an independent, self-contained entity. This is much like focusing on isolated decisions in the analysis of choice behavior or on isolated exchange in the study of bargaining. There is no doubt that this has certain advantages for initial efforts to understand behavioral prescriptions and the problem of compliance. Nevertheless, behavioral prescriptions typically occur in interrelated clusters. As an empirical generalization, it seems clear that what I described earlier in this essay as compliance systems are the rule rather than the exception in most societies.

[7] Even in the absence of information, compliant behavior may occur by chance. But such coincidences can hardly be counted upon to yield high levels of compliant behavior.

[8] Note, however, that in cases where high levels of compliance can be expected to follow from the dissemination of information, public authorities may find it less costly to expend resources on publicizing behavioral prescriptions than on punishing those who violate prescriptions out of ignorance.

A little reflection makes it clear that certain old problems become more severe and new problems emerge when we shift from the study of individual behavioral prescriptions to the analysis of compliance systems. Efforts to demarcate domain and scope are apt to be considerably more difficult. The constituent prescriptions in a compliance system often do not apply to precisely the same groups of subjects. Moreover, while a single prescription ordinarily requires some specified action, a compliance system will involve numerous actions and a wide range of appropriate circumstances. Consequently, there will often be ambiguities concerning who exactly is covered by a particular compliance system as well as when the relevant subjects are to act in the mode required.

Beyond this, the shift to compliance systems raises questions about internal consistency. Consider, for example, a system of grammar in which the following individual rules occur: (1) singular nouns *always* take singular verbs and (2) singular nouns referring to collective entities (for example, the government) take plural verbs. The inconsistency here is an obvious one. But many compliance systems contain more subtle inconsistencies, and the problems of identifying and resolving them can become serious in highly complex compliance systems. Finally, there is the prospect of particularly intractable conflicts between compliance systems. Imagine, for example, the problem faced by an individual who regards himself as subject to a system of professional norms requiring extremely high levels of professional achievement but who also sees himself as subject to a system of familial norms demanding the devotion of large amounts of time and energy to his family. In situations of this type, fully satisfactory solutions are often nonexistent and costly compromises become necessary.

Classifying behavioral prescriptions

There are several methods of classifying behavioral prescriptions which crop up frequently in discussions of compliance.[9] I shall comment on them briefly and express some tentative judgments on their utility for our purposes. First, there are different types of behavioral prescriptions. At the beginning of this section, I noted the distinctions among rules, laws, moral or ethical standards, and social norms. And it may well be possible to identify prescriptions that do not belong to any of these subdivisions. While it is obvious that these types of prescriptions differ significantly in some respects, it is not evident that these differences are of great importance from the point of view of compliance.

In a somewhat different vein, it is possible to distinguish among forms of behavioral prescriptions just as students of law commonly differentiate

[9] There is of course an unlimited number of ways in which a class of phenomena, such as behavioral prescriptions, can be classified. As with all taxonomies, the value of any given classification depends upon the purposes of those making the distinctions. See also the discussion entitled "Fundamentals of Taxonomy," in Hempel (1965, pp. 137–154).

various sources of law.[10] Thus, there are differences among prescriptions that are promulgated through some formal process, those that emerge from actual practice or custom, those that embody widely accepted or general principles of human behavior, and so forth. These comments also suggest a further distinction between written prescriptions and unwritten prescriptions.[11] Are subjects likely to respond differently to these various forms of behavioral prescriptions in making decisions about compliance? My preliminary judgment is that significant variations along these lines are probable, and I think this is an area that would repay more systematic research.

Next, there is a distinction between universal prescriptions and specialized prescriptions. This distinction refers both to domain and to scope. Thus, a universal prescription would be one applying to all actors under all conditions. A prescription to the effect that it is *never* acceptable to take a human life would fulfill these requirements. But in fact there are very few, if any, behavioral prescriptions in real-world situations which are universal.[12] For this reason, it is important to focus on specialized prescriptions, that is prescriptions that are more or less restricted with respect to domain or scope. Note, however, that the class of specialized prescriptions actually encompasses a wide range of possibilities. In this connection, it is common to classify behavioral prescriptions in terms of the functional area to which they pertain. For example, one might distinguish among social, economic, and political prescriptions or among educational, religious, and environmental prescriptions. To what extent are these functional distinctions useful for an understanding of compliance? Though it may well be desirable to pursue this question more systematically, my preliminary judgment is that these distinctions are not likely to prove crucial. The boundaries between functional areas are often highly artificial, and I am not aware of any evidence which indicates that compliance decisions vary significantly from one functional area to another.[13]

Beyond this, it is possible to classify behavioral prescriptions in terms of the frequency or iterativeness of the situations to which they pertain. Some behavioral prescriptions relate to situations that recur constantly in roughly the same form while others pertain to situations that occur only infrequently. Thus, a prescription specifying a highway speed limit is relevant every time a subject uses his automobile, but a prescription stating that certain actions should be taken to help a drowning person comes into

[10] For an exchange of views containing many suggestive comments on this subject see Hart (1958) and Fuller (1958).

[11] Unwritten prescriptions are of central importance in primitive societies. For a wealth of illustrative material consult Mair (1962) and Schapera (1967).

[12] Some prescriptions are meant to be universal in the sense of applying to all members of a given social system. But almost all behavioral prescriptions carry some contextual limitations that serve to restrict their scope.

[13] There are undoubtedly differences in behavior among types of actors. Insofar as functional divisions correlate with differences among types of actors, therefore, we can expect to observe variations in compliance behavior from one functional area to another.

play quite infrequently. I believe this distinction is of considerable importance to public authorities contemplating what sorts of institutional arrangements to introduce to encourage compliant behavior in specific situations. Actions required of large groups of subjects with great frequency may justify the introduction of far more elaborate and extensive compliance mechanisms than actions required in conjunction with highly uncommon situations.

Finally, there is a widespread distinction between positive (or compellent) prescriptions and negative (or deterrent) prescriptions. Briefly, a positive prescription is one requiring subjects to take certain concrete actions under specified circumstances while a negative prescription is one proscribing various actions under specified circumstances. It is often asserted that it is more difficult to elicit compliance with positive prescriptions than with negative prescriptions. This assertion rests on a critical premise concerning the locus of initiative. Positive prescriptions require subjects to initiate well-defined actions whereas negative prescriptions merely require inaction. The critical premise is that it will generally be easier to get subjects to refrain from doing something than to induce them actually to take positive steps. There is no doubt that this is a subject requiring further investigation,[14] but my tentative judgment is that this distinction does have important implications for the achievement of compliance in concrete situations.

Behavioral prescriptions vs. other rules

Though the category of behavioral prescriptions is an extensive one, it does not encompass all rules or laws relating to human behavior. For example, the proposition that individual entrepreneurs act to maximize profits is a law-like statement but it is not one that belongs to the category of behavioral prescriptions. If, on the other hand, I assert that individuals should always pay their income tax on time, I am dealing with matters pertaining to the category of behavioral prescriptions. These examples suggest that several more conceptual distinctions will shed additional light on the concept.

To begin with, it is worth differentiating behavioral prescriptions from universal or general laws. General laws assert constant links (i.e. conjunctions or disjunctions) between specifiable empirical phenomena whereas behavioral prescriptions spell out links between stated circumstances and normatively prescribed actions (Hempel, 1966, chap. 5). Thus, general laws are empirical rather than normative statements, and of course they occur in many areas having nothing to do with human behavior. For example, the statement that the distance a freely falling body traverses is proportional to the square of the time of its fall (Galileo's law) is a well-known

---

[14] For an extensive comparison of the concepts "compellence" and "deterrence" see Schelling (1966, pp. 69–91). A discussion that raises some searching questions about the conception of compellence and deterrence presented here appears in Baldwin (1976).

law, but it has no relevance to the concept of behavioral prescriptions. If a general law is valid and its contextual limitations are properly stated, it will not be subject to violation.[15] By contrast, it is precisely the possibility of violations on the part of the relevant subjects which gives rise to the problem of compliance in connection with behavioral prescriptions.

It may also help to distinguish behavioral prescriptions from what I shall call guidelines. A behavioral prescription is a normatively compelling guide to action. A guideline, by contrast, is a practical guide offering advice on the preferred or most efficient method of achieving some goal. The injunction against taking human life, for example, is a prescription, whereas the statement that the oil in an automobile should be changed every six months to ensure good performance and minimize deterioration is a guideline. Both prescriptions and guidelines can be violated in specific situations, and there are apt to be penalties associated with violations in both cases.[16] But violating a prescription involves disregarding a normative injunction while ignoring a guideline is simply a matter of rejecting advice which it might have paid to heed.

Finally, I want to comment on the relationship between behavioral prescriptions and rights. Behavioral prescriptions are guides to action; rights are entitlements arising from the occupancy of a given role (for example, citizen, property holder, patient).[17] In a sense, rights and prescriptions constitute the opposite sides of a coin. The existence of a right signifies the absence of a prescription concerning a given issue. Nevertheless, the exercise of rights is often limited by prescriptions. For example, the right to free speech is limited by the prescription against speaking in such a way as to incite a riot. Further, prescriptions are sometimes introduced as a means of securing rights. Thus, prescriptions against theft play an important role in securing the property rights of those who own private property. Accordingly, the relationship between rights and prescriptions is a close one (von Wright, 1963).

COMPLIANCE

In simple situations, the phenomenon of compliance presents few conceptual difficulties. Compliance can be said to occur when the actual behavior of a given subject conforms to prescribed behavior, and noncompliance or violation occurs when actual behavior departs significantly from prescribed behavior. Moreover, it is easy to measure levels of com-

---

[15] Of course, a law-like assertion may ultimately be falsified. But so long as it is accepted as a valid law, it is not meaningful to think in terms of its being violated.

[16] It follows from this discussion that guidelines bear a relationship to what is sometimes called prescriptive theory in contrast to descriptive theory. For a clear statement of this distinction see Rapoport (1964, pp. 5–6).

[17] Though the category of rights is a broad one, the concept has been developed most rigorously in connection with property rights. For a survey of literature in this area see Furubotn and Pejovich (1972).

pliance in such simple situations. The level of compliance exhibited by a subject or a group of subjects is simply the ratio of actual compliant acts to the total number of possible compliant acts. Conversely, the level of violation is the ratio of actual violations to the total number of possible violations. However, the concept of compliance becomes considerably more complex as we move away from the simplest types of situations. In this section, therefore, I want to examine some conceptual complexities associated with the problem of compliance as it actually arises in most real-world situations.

Is compliance a binary choice?

People commonly think of the choice problem faced by the subject of a behavioral prescription as a simple matter of deciding between clear-cut compliance and clear-cut violation. It is undoubtedly easy and convenient to think of compliance as a binary choice, but I believe that it is unsatisfactory. There are numerous cases in which some sort of partial compliance is possible. For example, firms may engage in half-hearted efforts to comply with emission control standards. And many employers are willing to take some steps toward ending sex discrimination without engaging in an all-out effort to do so. Of course, the relevant public authorities will have some control over the extent to which partial compliance is feasible in most situations. But there can be no doubt that partial compliance is a prominent phenomenon in many real-world situations.

In addition, it is often possible for subjects to exhibit ambiguous, dilatory, or confusing behavior in conjunction with compliance problems. Thus, compliance can be claimed by a subject under conditions which are difficult to verify (for example, a claim that arms have not been produced clandestinely while external inspection is rejected). A subject can assert that he actually performed a given act but that the relevant public authority failed to observe him doing it or to record the event. Or a subject can claim that his attorney or accountant failed to carry out his instructions relating to the prescription in question. In all these cases, the basic idea is to take steps whose purpose is to make it difficult to tell whether a subject has complied with or violated a given behavioral prescription.

There are some situations in which it is even possible to respond to behavioral prescriptions in probabilistic rather than determinate terms. For example, a subject may decide whether or not to leave his automobile in a no parking zone by applying some arbitrary decision rule such as flipping a coin. What considerations would lead a subject to behave in this fashion? In general, the use of expected value calculations may make probabilistic responses emerge as the rational course of action for subjects facing certain types of compliance problems (Rapoport, 1964, pp. 12–30). Further, subjects may hope to profit from actions of this sort by catching public authorities off guard and unprepared to deal with their behavior.

In most cases, the extent to which a given compliance problem is formulated in binary terms will be a function of the gradual evolution of per-
ceptions and attitudes over time or of the deliberate policy of the relevant
public authority toward the prescription in question. Under these circumstances, the issue of binary choice becomes a decision variable rather than
a matter beyond human control. Will public authorities generally find it
advantageous to pose compliance problems to their subjects in strict binary
terms? A little reflection suggests that they will often experience cross-
pressures. Binary formulations have the advantage of making it easier to
detect violations since it is possible to argue that any action that does not
clearly constitute compliance with a given prescription necessarily involves
a violation of some kind. On the other hand, binary formulations will
often push subjects toward the commission of particularly costly and
dangerous violations. If all the intermediate alternatives are eliminated and
if the subject cannot accept the consequences of complying with a given
prescription, he will have no choice but to become an outright violator.
Consequently, though the extent to which a given prescription is posed as
a matter of binary choice will typically be subject to manipulation, public
authorities will want to consider this question carefully before adopting
any specific posture.

Some additional complexities

Even in cases where compliance appears to be largely a matter of binary
choice, there are other complications that ensure that it does not become
a cut-and-dried issue. Here are several prominent examples. It is one thing
for an actor to accept a behavioral prescription as authoritative, legitimate,
or desirable within the context of his social system. It is another thing to
decide actually to comply with the requirements of the prescription in
specific situations. In fact, there are sometimes good reasons for an actor
to regard the existence of a particular prescription as desirable and yet
deliberately to violate the prescription himself. This is apt to occur when
the actor expects the majority of the other members of the social system
to comply with the requirements of the prescription. Under such conditions, the actor may hope to enjoy the benefits accruing to a successful
"free rider." That is, he can hope to receive the benefits of an orderly social system flowing from the compliant behavior of others while reaping the
benefits stemming from his own violations at the same time. For example,
if I expect others to abide faithfully by the rule that promises should be
kept, it may occur to me that I can reap certain gains by breaking this
rule myself.[18]

Next, suppose that you definitely do not wish to comply with a given
behavioral prescription but that you also want to avoid the appearance

---

[18] Such behavior is also likely to be affected by attitudes toward strategic interaction.
For differing perspectives in this area consult Lewis (1969, pp. 24–51) and Young
(1975, Introduction).

of being an outright violator. Imagine also that the compliance problem has been posed initially as a matter of binary choice. In fact, there are several techniques that are sometimes useful in efforts to avoid the appearance of outright violation in such situations. You can make claims based on the doctrine of *rebus sic stantibus*.[19] That is, you can assert that the prescription in question is not authoritative under the circumstances at hand for one reason or another, or that conditions have changed so drastically over time that the prescription is outmoded and no longer applicable. Another possibility is to argue that the public authority or someone else has defined the situation improperly and that it does not actually involve an application of the behavioral prescription it superficially appears to involve. For example, you may claim that a given action does not actually involve a breach of contract on the grounds that the contract in question was not drawn up properly at the outset and is consequently not to be regarded as legally binding. Going a step further, subjects may attempt simply to redefine the situation in order to avoid the necessity of making a clear-cut choice between compliance and violation. To illustrate: if a country wishes to intervene in a conflict taking place within another country without appearing to violate the rule against intervention in internal conflicts, it can claim that the situation really amounts to a case of international warfare rather than civil strife (Falk, 1964). All these practices are widespread in real-world situations, especially in social systems lacking authoritative procedures to resolve disputes about the precise nature of compliance situations.

A further complication arises from the distinction between the "letter" and the "spirit" of a prescription (Fuller, 1969). There are many situations in which it is possible to circumvent the intent of behavioral prescriptions without violating them in any formal sense. Clever entrepreneurs, for example, have found many ways of placing restraints on trade without formally violating the provisions of antitrust legislation. Similarly, states have often acted in such a way as to prevent the achievement of the basic goals of arms control agreements even while complying with the formal provisions of these agreements. Problems of this kind appear to be widespread in all social systems.

The comments in the preceding paragraphs refer to situations in which a subject wishes to avoid complying with some behavioral prescription. Conversely, cases often arise in which it is difficult to prove conclusively to others that you are in fact complying with a given prescription even when you are quite prepared to do so (Schelling, 1960, pp. 43–46). This is sometimes attributable to problems of verifying intangible phenomena. For example, it may be difficult for me to prove to you that I do not harbor any racial prejudices, if you are not prepared to take my word for it. In other cases, the problem arises from the fact that the necessary forms

---

[19] The doctrine of *rebus sic stantibus* has been developed most explicitly and extensively in the field of international law (Brierly, 1963, pp. 335–341).

of verification are politically unacceptable. Thus, it may be extremely difficult for a given country to prove that it is not producing fissionable material in the absence of external inspections that are quite unacceptable (Falk and Barnet, 1965, part I). Beyond this, there are many situations in which the costs of demonstrating that you are complying with a prescription are unusually high. A classic illustration involves the problem of safeguarding industrial secrets while revealing enough information to prove compliance with safety standards, environmental regulations, and other industrial rules. In all these situations, actors will have a definite interest in the development of methods through which actual compliance can be demonstrated at an acceptable cost in terms of other values. In some cases, actors will even be willing to pay a substantial price for such arrangements, and they may find it profitable to invest resources in research and development in this area.[20] Such incentives will be especially strong in cases where the action in question is highly iterative or the costs of noncompliance are unusually high.

Indicators of compliance

In some cases, the occurrence of compliance or noncompliance with a behavioral prescription is self-evident. It is not difficult to tell whether the rule that the lights in the hospital ward are to be turned off at 9 pm is being violated. Similarly, there is no problem in ascertaining whether automobile owners are complying with a law requiring them to attach new license plates to their automobiles by some specified deadline. But it is far more difficult to determine whether subjects are in fact complying with many other behavioral prescriptions. Sometimes this is due to the problem of operationality I described earlier. For example, how is one to determine whether a banker is violating a law prohibiting sex discrimination in decisions about loans? In other cases, the problem arises from the high cost of obtaining the necessary information. Thus, it is often difficult to check on compliance with emission control standards designed to reduce air pollution because of the high cost of isolating and assessing carefully the activities of a particular business firm or enterprise.[21]

These difficulties typically give rise to a search by public authorities for what I shall call indicators of compliance. An indicator of compliance is a simple observable measure that can plausibly be regarded as signalling whether or not a subject is complying with the requirements of a given prescription. Thus, the regular occurrence of close scores may be taken as evidence that the norm of fair play is being observed in competitive sports. The presence of roughly equal numbers of men and women in a given line of work may be regarded as an indicator of compliance with laws prohibiting sex discrimination. And the regular performance of religious rituals is

---

[20] One way to avoid the problem of demonstrating compliance is to engage in some form of collusion with the relevant public authority.

[21] For one interesting response to problems of this kind see Dales (1968).

sometimes treated as an indicator that an individual is complying with the more intangible moral precepts associated with the religion in question. In each of these cases, the use of a simple indicator substantially resolves the initial problem of checking on compliance with specific behavioral prescriptions. But note that the indicators themselves are actually surrogate measures of compliance.

This can generate severe problems that make it doubtful whether the benefits flowing from the introduction of such indicators outweigh the costs. Consider, for example, the use of simple ratios as indicators of compliance with laws prohibiting sex discrimination in employment. On the one hand, *pro forma* compliance as measured by this type of indicator in no way demonstrates that the underlying attitudes and biases associated with sex discrimination have been eliminated. It is perfectly possible to manifest a variety of more subtle forms of discrimination even while complying with indicators in the form of formal ratios. At the same time, reliance on indicators of this type may well produce new problems whose consequences are unfortunate. The use of sex ratios in employment, for example, could lead to the hiring of unqualified persons as well as the rejection of qualified persons.

Social costs

In examining compliance decisions of individual subjects, it is natural to focus on the costs and benefits of compliance (vs. violation) to the individuals themselves. There can be little doubt that individuals make choices about compliance in an essentially self-interested fashion in the sense that they consider only the discernible impacts of their choices on themselves and will not devote much thought to the impact of those choices on the welfare of others (Frohlich, 1974). Nor will an individual spend much time contemplating the social implications of his choices under various assumptions about the behavior of other members of his group.

Nevertheless, when whole groups of individuals make choices about compliance with behavioral prescriptions, problems relating to social costs inevitably arise. The set of individual choices, taken together, will have significant consequences for the social system as a whole. It is, therefore, meaningful to raise questions about the social costs, in contrast to the individual costs, of various aggregate levels of violation in a given social system. One way to think about these issues is to turn to the concept of Pareto optimality. Having ascertained the existing level of violations in a given social system with respect to a particular behavioral prescription or set of prescriptions, we can ask whether some lower or higher level of violations would be Pareto superior to the existing level. This is equivalent to asking whether a shift to some alternative level of violations would make at least one member of the group better off without making any member of the group worse off.

However, the criterion of Pareto optimality is not likely to be of much help in most real-world situations involving compliance. This is so because most changes in the aggregate level of violations will have negative consequences for the welfare of at least some members of the social system even though they are beneficial for others. That is, almost all possible outcomes will be Pareto optimal. Consequently, it is necessary to think about other approaches to the phenomenon of social costs in the realm of compliance. I suggest that it is useful to think about these costs in terms of the relationship between aggregate levels of violations on the one hand and overall quality of life on the other.[22] There are of course obvious problems in using the concept of quality of life since it does not seem possible to reduce this notion readily to a straightforward monetary dimension or simple utility measure (Mishan, 1967). Therefore, the use of this approach suggests the need for a good deal of additional research.

Nevertheless, I think it is possible even at this stage to introduce some reasonable assumptions about the relationship between social costs (measured in terms of the expected value of quality of life) and aggregate levels of violations. First, social costs will be zero when the aggregate level of violations is also zero, that is in the presence of perfect compliance. There may in fact be cases in which social costs remain effectively at the zero point even given the presence of low aggregate levels of violations. Second, once social costs arise at all they will increase continuously as a function of increases in the aggregate level of violations (or reductions in the level of compliance). Third, the relationship between social costs and the aggregate level of violations will not be linear. There will generally be increasing marginal social costs as a function of increasing aggregate levels of violations (or decreasing levels of compliance), though there may be special cases in which this relationship exhibits some other form over certain ranges.

Individuals may not need to or even be able to worry much about the problem of social costs. In most cases, they will have their hands full making their own choices about compliance without thinking explicitly about the issue of social costs. At the same time, there is no doubt that public authorities will generally find it necessary to devote a good deal of attention to the problem of social costs. This does not arise from any devotion to the "public interest" by public authorities. Rather, it stems directly from the fact that the level of social costs arising from noncompliant behavior will play a key role in determining whether an existing public authority can continue to function effectively in any given social system.

[22] In extreme cases, the aggregate level of violations may reach a point where social collapse occurs. By social collapse, I mean a condition in which the implicit social contract governing the behavior of the members of a social system is no longer operative. Accordingly, social collapse constitutes a special, and extreme, case of deterioration in the quality of life in a social system.

CHAPTER 7

The behavior of public authorities

Though I have often referred to public authorities, I have so far avoided a systematic examination of their behavior. Now I want to confront this issue. What goals should public authorities pursue in the realm of compliance and how can they best utilize their resources to achieve these goals? What objectives do public authorities in fact pursue in this realm and how do they make investment decisions regarding compliance mechanisms?

THE NATURE OF PUBLIC AUTHORITIES

A public authority is defined here as an institutional arrangement that is vested with the task of eliciting compliance with some set of behavioral prescriptions in an identifiable social system. Such an arrangement may be formalized in a constitution, but formalization is not a defining characteristic of public authorities. Nor is such formalization a necessary condition for success in the efforts of public authorities to elicit compliance from subject groups.[1]

In thinking about public authorities, we are apt to focus immediately on formal and relatively centralized institutions like governments. While governments undoubtedly are classic examples of the category, public authorities encompass institutional arrangements going well beyond the standard conception of government. Some public authorities are highly specialized with respect to the range of behavioral prescriptions they deal with, while others are much broader. Some authorities focus entirely on a single substantive area such as air and water pollution or marine fisheries.[2]

---

[1] A striking case in point is the government of the United Kingdom, which does *not* operate under the terms of a formal constitution.

[2] For a case study of one such agency see Haas (1958).

Similarly, public authorities vary greatly in the extent to which they evolve as informal arrangements or as highly formalized institutions. For example, arrangements known as "invisible colleges" operate to elicit compliance with the norms of scientific research on a highly informal basis, while enforcement agencies in the realm of criminal behavior are typically highly formalized. Finally, and most important, public authorities vary greatly with respect to centralization. Though formal governments may seem like the norm, it is possible to set up periodic conferences or loosely structured commissions, in which most of the day-to-day tasks involved in the achievement of compliance are delegated to individual members of the social system (Burke, Legatski, and Woodhead, 1975).

How do public authorities behave in the realm of compliance? In this chapter, I shall assume that public authorities dealing with compliance resemble the profit-maximizing firms of microeconomics (Henderson and Quandt, 1958).[3] First, they will approach the issue of compliance as an investment problem. That is, they will attempt to maximize returns from the investment of resources in compliance mechanisms. And they will be concerned with the opportunity costs of investing resources in the achievement of compliance, since they will always face situations involving numerous other demands on available resources. Second, investment decisions relating to compliance will generally be important enough to be made consciously. This is an important source of differences between the behavior of public authorities and the behavior of individual actors in the realm of compliance. Third, public authorities will systematically weigh the costs and benefits of investing in compliance mechanisms. While I do not assume that they will always be able to compute these costs and benefits in monetary terms, I do assume that they will be able to make relatively powerful assumptions about such costs and benefits for the purposes of proceeding with investment decisions. Fourth, public authorities will be marginalists in the sense that they will invest resources in compliance mechanisms until the marginal cost of the last unit of resources invested just equals the marginal benefit stemming from that unit.[4] That is, they will reach equilibrium with respect to investments in compliance mechanisms where marginal costs are equal to marginal revenue.[5]

[3] It will no doubt prove necessary to modify this conception significantly when it comes to the examination of highly decentralized public authorities, but I am convinced that this perspective constitutes a good starting point.

[4] For a clear discussion of the principles of marginal analysis consult Henderson and Quandt (1958).

[5] Several subsidiary issues deserve mention in passing. It is important to remember that there will always be numerous demands on the resources of public authorities other than those associated with problems of compliance. Consequently, public authorities will experience inherent pressures to accept optim'stic assumptions about the performance of specific compliance mechanisms and to cut corners on the cost of compliance mechanisms wherever possible. Beyond this, public authorities seldom start with a clean slate in the realm of compliance. That is, they rarely find themselves in the position of

A NORMATIVE MODEL

Given these assumptions, how will public authorities proceed in the realm of compliance? The crucial issue here concerns the computation of the relevant costs and benefits. I propose to begin with the development of a normative model, leaving questions concerning its empirical applicability to the next section of this chapter.

The computation of costs associated with the development and operation of compliance mechanisms is a relatively straightforward matter. Briefly, these costs will be treated as are other expenditures of scarce resources; compliance mechanisms require equipment, training, the time of personnel, and so forth. The total pool of resources available to the public authority is finite, and compliance is only one of the areas in which it will invest resources. Therefore, opportunity costs will play the same role with respect to compliance mechanisms that they play in other areas.

The real problem is in computing the benefits arising from the investment of resources in compliance mechanisms. I shall, for the time being, adopt the normative postulate that public authorities calculate these benefits in terms of reductions in those social costs that arise from violations of behavioral prescriptions. This assumes that the quality of life for the members of a society will be negatively affected by a rising level of violations.[6] While it is difficult to reduce these costs to straightforward monetary measures, it is possible, as I suggested in chapter 6, to formulate general propositions about the connection between social costs and violations. For the moment, I shall assume that public authorities regard the reduction of social costs as the principal source of benefits arising from the investment of resources in compliance mechanisms.

Under these conditions, what can we say about the question of how much a given public authority will invest in compliance mechanisms? As I have formulated it, this problem lends itself to graphical analysis of the type employed in microeconomics. Figure 1 portrays the situation facing our public authority as it contemplates a particular compliance problem. The X axis of this graph represents the percentage of violations or noncompliant acts. It is the ratio of actual violations to potential violations of a particular prescription for a given population or subject group.

---

starting from scratch and selecting a whole new program of compliance mechanisms. On the contrary, most choices in this realm involve incremental changes: whether to allocate a little more or a little less to compliance mechanisms during the next time period or whether it is worth adding one new compliance mechanism to the repertory of mechanisms already in use. None of this reduces the relevance of the basic pattern of marginal calculations outlined in the text. But these observations may help to forestall some common misconceptions about the behavior of public authorities with respect to compliance.

6 Note the difference between this usage of the phrase "social costs" and the usage that is common among economists (Pigou, 1932, pp. 131–135). The social costs arising from noncompliance are discussed further in chapter 6 *supra*.

Costs

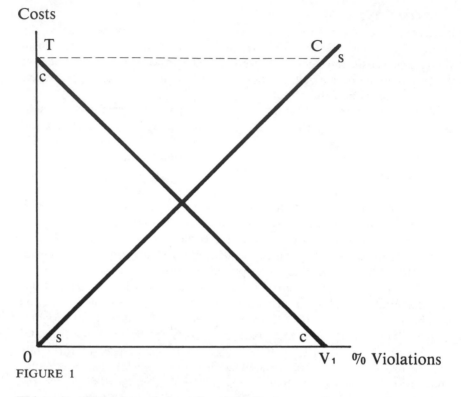

FIGURE 1

This axis will be bounded on the right. It cannot take on a value greater than 1, which would occur if every member of the subject group engaged in noncompliant behavior at all times. The Y axis represents two types of costs (measured in terms of a common numeraire).[7] On the one hand, it is an indicator of the social costs stemming from the occurrence of violations or noncompliant behavior. At the same time, this axis represents expenditures of resources by the public authority on compliance mechanisms (that is, compliance costs). Going up the Y axis, then, involves increases both in social and compliance costs.

The curve labeled *ss* in figure 1 is a social cost curve. It maps the social cost associated with each level of compliance or noncompliance in the system, and its slope at any given point is a measure of marginal social costs. The *cc* curve is essentially a production function. It indicates the level of compliance (that is, the reciprocal of the percentage of violations) that can be obtained for any given level of expenditure of resources on compliance mechanisms. Accordingly, the slope of the *cc* curve measures the marginal productivity of investing resources in compliance mechanisms.

[7] That is, I assume that it is possible to identify some unit of measure that is suitable for measuring both social costs and compliance costs. Beyond this, however, I assume only that this unit of measure can serve as the basis for an interval scale.

The curves in figure 1 are drawn in accordance with several assumptions. First, in the absence of any violations (that is, in the case of perfect compliance), social costs are 0. Second, the first units of compliance are free goods. That is, the cc curve intersects the X axis to the left of its righthand boundary.[8] Third, the slopes of the two curves are constant. This means that marginal social costs and marginal compliance costs are not increasing or decreasing. Fourth, the slopes of the two curves are equal and opposite. Taken together, these assumptions identify a highly restricted special case, a fact that will become apparent in the ensuing discussion.

The function TC is a measure of the *total costs* considered by the public authority at any given level of violations and expenditures on compliance mechanisms. Total costs are the sum of social costs and compliance costs at each specified level of operations. Formally, $TC(v_i) = ss_{v_i} + cc_{v_i}$, and TC will obviously vary as a function of ss and cc.

Now, what is the rational course of action for the public authority under these conditions?[9] The answer is clear: the public authority will always attempt to minimize total costs. That is, TC_{min} will constitute the point of equilibrium with respect to the public authority's investments in compliance mechanisms. This is because, in order to make such investments worthwhile, the gains to be had from the last bit of reduction in social costs must more than offset the compliance costs of achieving that reduction. So long as this condition prevails, it will be possible to reduce total costs below their current level, and the public authority will find it profitable to make the necessary investment. Accordingly, TC_{min} is the point where marginal costs equal marginal revenue for a public authority operating on the basis of the assumptions set forth in the preceding paragraphs.

At this point, we are ready to examine a number of specific cases which are compatible with the model I have been developing, and to consider the implications of these cases for the behavior of public authorities contemplating investments in compliance mechanisms. I shall begin with linear cases; that is, those cases in which the slopes of the ss and cc curves are constant over their entire range. Three cases of this type are of obvious interest in this discussion.

To begin with, there is the case in which the slopes of the ss and cc curves are equal and opposite. This is the case portrayed in figure 1. The salient features of this case are as follows: TC is constant over the whole range from 0 to v_1 (which is the point where the cc curve intersects the X axis). In addition, the marginal costs and marginal revenues associated with investments in compliance mechanisms are equal and invariant

[8] This means that subjects will comply with some behavioral prescriptions even in the absence of external sanctions. Other incentives for compliance, such as self-interest and feelings of obligation, are discussed in chapter 2.

[9] In this discussion, I assume that the public authority has the information required to make computations of social costs and compliance costs.

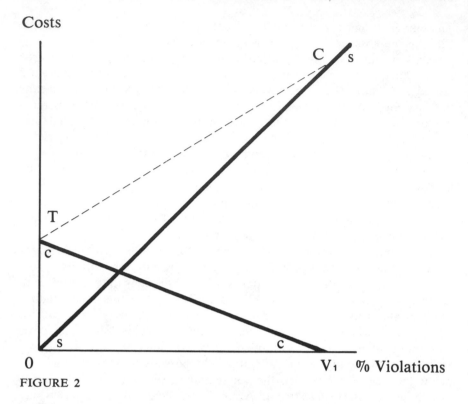

FIGURE 2

throughout this whole range. Both these results flow directly from the fact that the slopes of the *ss* and *cc* curves are constant, equal, and opposite. The policy implications of this situation are readily apparent: the public authority will be indifferent concerning expenditures of resources on compliance mechanisms at all levels. That is, it makes no difference how much is expended on compliance mechanisms; the overall result from the point of view of the public authority will be the same regardless of its investment level. In such cases, public authorities would have to make their decisions in terms of some criterion exogenous to our model.[10]

Now consider another linear case in which the slope of the *ss* curve is greater than the slope of the *cc* curve throughout. As figure 2 indicates, this means that the *ss* curve is always steeper than the *cc* curve. Under these conditions, marginal revenues derived from the reduction of violations will exceed marginal compliance costs everywhere to the left of v_1, and *TC* will decline continuously as more resources are invested in compliance mechanisms. The public policy implication of this is that the public authority will find it profitable to go on investing in compliance mechan-

---

[10] Such decisions might rest on cultural norms, rules of thumb, or procedural devices like rolling dice.

Costs

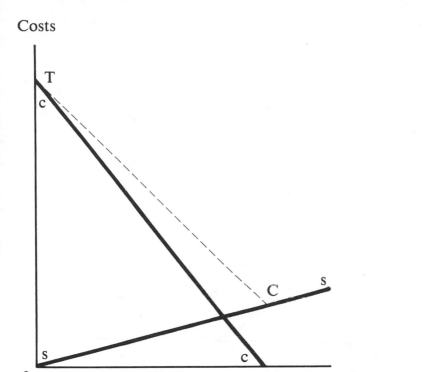

FIGURE 3

isms until violations are eliminated altogether. This is a reflection of the fact that figure 2 depicts a situation in which violations bring serious social costs while the compliance costs of reducing violations are moderate throughout.

The last of the linear cases is the reverse of the situation portrayed in figure 2. That is, the slope of the ss curve is less than the slope of the cc curve throughout. As would be expected, the marginal costs of investing in compliance mechanisms exceed the marginal gains from reduced violations at all points to the left of v_1, and TC increases continuously over this range. Accordingly, TC_{min} occurs precisely at v_1, and the rational public authority will make no effort to develop compliance mechanisms to reduce violations. Again, this is a consequence of the fact that the case portrayed in figure 3 is one in which it is expensive to control violations while the social costs associated with violations are not especially severe. The overall conclusion to be drawn from this discussion so far, therefore, is that it is not possible to assert either that public authorities will always try to cut down violations as far as possible or that these authorities will always ignore prospects for controlling violations.

Costs

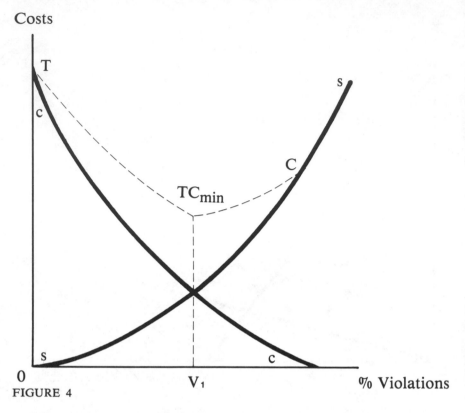

FIGURE 4

The preceding discussion focuses exclusively on situations in which the slopes of the *ss* and *cc* curves are constant. But there is no reason to suppose that real-world conditions will typically conform to this assumption of linearity. On the contrary, linearities along these lines will be uncommon in the real world. Figure 4 depicts the general situation I would expect to encounter in most real-world situations. This case is characterized both by increasing marginal social costs and by increasing marginal compliance costs. That is, social costs rise more and more rapidly as a function of the level of violations or noncompliant behavior in the social system. Similarly, the incremental costs of obtaining additional units of compliance go up as the overall level of compliance rises. The first thing to notice about this case is that there is no longer a corner solution as there was in each of the two previous cases. Nevertheless, the public authority will certainly not be indifferent about levels of investment in compliance mechanisms; initial investments in such mechanisms yield reductions in *TC*, though this situation will turn around well before perfect compliance is achieved. In the case portrayed in figure 4, TC_{min} occurs at the point labeled v_1, but the locus of TC_{min} in other cases of this type will be a function of the exact shapes of the *ss* and *cc* curves. More generally, we can conclude that

Costs

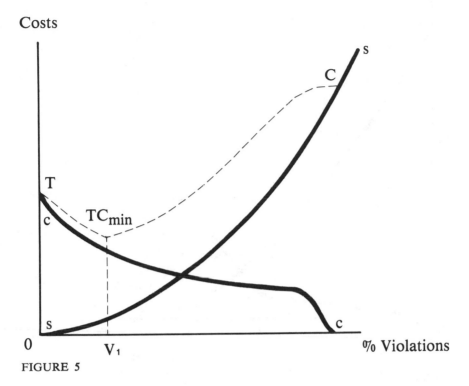

FIGURE 5

under the conditions assumed in this paragraph (1) public authorities will find it profitable to invest in compliance mechanisms, and (2) they will reach equilibrium with respect to their investments in these mechanisms before eliminating noncompliant behavior altogether.

It is evident that there are numerous variations on the theme of nonlinear cost curves, and it would be tedious to explore them all in this discussion.[11] Nevertheless, it seems fruitful to look at several of these variations in order to indicate something of the range of interesting possibilities. In this connection, consider first a case in which there are significant economies of scale in the production of compliance. This phenomenon is depicted in figure 5, in which the *ss* curve is identical to that in figure 4 but in which the per unit cost of producing additional units of compliance actually declines over a lengthy range. The basic effect of this variation is to shift the locus of TC_{min} to the left and downward. That is, the public authority will now find it possible to obtain a higher level of compliance even while making a saving in terms of total costs. This outcome is of course intuitively appealing since this is the impact we would expect from the occurrence of economies of scale.

---

[11] The exact shapes of these curves will be sensitive to numerous special features of concrete compliance problems.

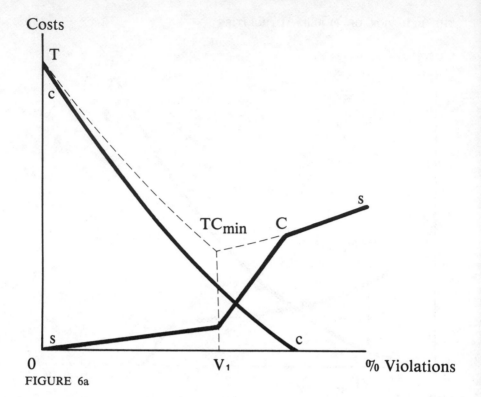

FIGURE 6a

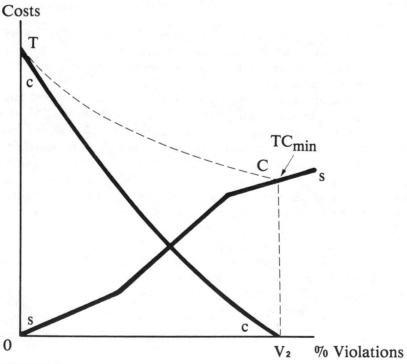

FIGURE 6b

120

A rather different result emerges from an examination of the situation portrayed in figure 6. This case is characterized by the occurrence of a sharp flex in the social cost curve. The idea here is that there are situations in which social costs increase gradually up to a certain threshold of violations but rise abruptly thereafter. This possibility may well be relevant in some real-world situations. The consequences of this variation depend critically on the locus of the point of inflection in the ss curve. The cc curves in figure 6a and 6b are identical, but the point of inflection in the ss curve comes much earlier in 6b than in 6a. Under these circumstances, the public authority will find it clearly worthwhile to invest in compliance mechanisms in 6a (TC_{min} occurs at the point labeled v_1), but it will have no incentive to invest in such mechanisms when it faces the situation portrayed in 6b (TC rises continuously from v_2, which is the point at which the cc curve intersects the X axis). It is clear, then, that the exact shapes of the cost curves in nonlinear cases can play a critical role in determining the choices of rational public authorities with respect to investments in compliance mechanisms.

It is also worth emphasizing that several factors other than the shapes of the cost curves will capture the attention of public authorities in situations of the type under discussion. Two simple examples will make this point clear. Imagine that a public authority discovers that it can produce compliance with some behavioral prescriptions more cheaply by orchestrating and encouraging various forms of social pressure than by making use of standard techniques of enforcement and inducement.[12] Figure 7 illustrates this case. The curve c_1c_1 maps compliance costs when the public authority relies solely on enforcement, while c_2c_2 maps the same costs when the authority makes use of social pressures. Under these conditions, a public authority relying solely on enforcement would not find it worthwhile to invest in compliance mechanisms. But the same authority exploiting social pressures would find such an investment profitable to the point where violations were eliminated altogether. Moreover, the total costs would be or_1 if the authority were to think only in terms of enforcement but only or_2 if it pursued a program of social pressures. Fundamentally, this difference arises from the slopes of the two compliance cost curves rather than from their shapes.

Looking at the intercepts of the cost curves on the axes of our graphs, it is quite easy to demonstrate that the intercept of the cc curve on the X axis will not affect the basic policy decisions of a rational public authority, though it may have a substantial impact on the total costs associated with the decisions of the authority. To see this, consider the situation depicted in figure 8. In 8a, c_1c_1 intersects the X axis far to the right of c_2c_2. But in both cases, the public authority will find it profitable to invest in compli-

---

[12] The idea here is that social pressures, of the type discussed in chapter 2, can sometimes be exploited or molded by a public authority interested in maximizing the amount of compliance obtained for each unit of resources invested.

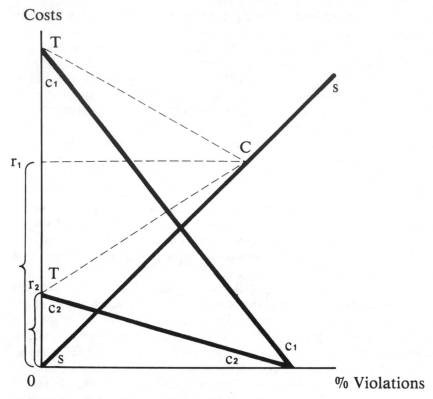

FIGURE 7

ance mechanisms to the point of eliminating violations altogether. Now consider 8b. Here c_3c_3 intersects the X axis far to the right of c_4c_4, and the authority will not be moved to invest any resources in compliance mechanisms in either case. Thus, the intercept of cc on the X axis clearly does not alter basic policy decisions on the part of public authorities, but it will affect the total costs associated with problems of compliance. So, we have the difference between or_1 and or_2 in 8a, and the gap between or_3 and or_4 in 8b. This means only that, other things being equal, total costs will be lower when substantial amounts of compliance can be obtained without cost to the public authority than when the authority can count on very little compliance in the absence of investments in compliance mechanisms.[13]

So far, I have been examining cases involving a particular problem of compliance. But many public authorities will have to cope with sets of compliance problems simultaneously. What happens when a public authority proceeds to aggregate across issue areas? In my judgment, the major effects of aggregation are likely to be those portrayed in figure 9, in which

[13] The amount of compliance forthcoming without cost to the public authority will be a function of the strength of the various incentives (other than enforcement and inducement) discussed in chapter 2.

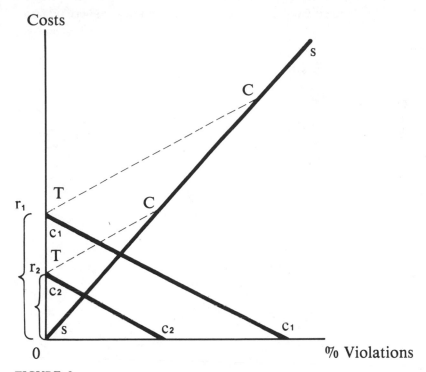

FIGURE 8a

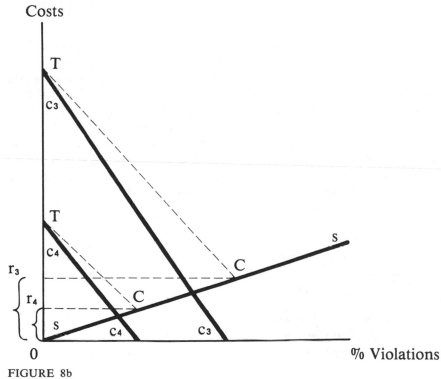

FIGURE 8b

123

Costs

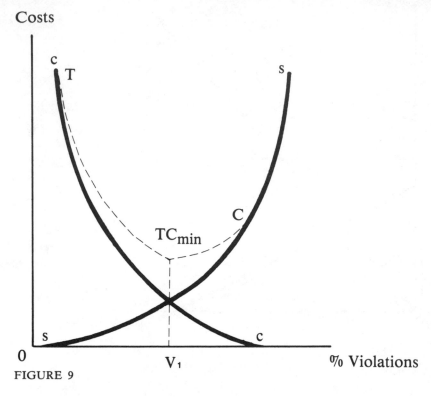

FIGURE 9

we treat the *cc* and *ss* curves as aggregate measures of compliance costs and social costs, respectively. Two features of this situation are particularly noteworthy. First, perfect compliance is infeasible. In other words, the cost of eliminating the last elements of noncompliance is infinite, and the *cc* curve eventually becomes asymptotic to the Y axis. Second, at some point social costs blow up and become infinite. This means that the social system will collapse somewhere before the point of completely noncompliant behavior by the whole population with respect to all relevant problems of compliance. The significance of these features is entirely straightforward. They ensure that the public authority will always find it profitable to make some investment in compliance mechanisms. But equally, they guarantee that the public authority will never find it worthwhile to endeavor to eliminate violations altogether in the aggregate. To the extent that these conditions are realistic, then, we can expect public authorities to be active in the development of compliance mechanisms but to reach equilibrium well before the point of perfect compliance.

WHAT PUBLIC AUTHORITIES ACTUALLY DO

How realistic are the basic conditions embedded in the model developed in the preceding section? This query raises two sets of issues. First, the behavior of many public authorities is the result of complex internal social choice processes rather than coordinated and rational decision making (see chapter 3 for a discussion of the implications of this). On the other hand, when public authorities are more or less coordinated entities, it is important to realize that they are likely to be motivated by some form of self-interest (Frohlich, Oppenheimer, and Young, 1971, especially chap. 2).

The critical issue in this connection concerns the empirical applicability of the normative assumptions made in the preceding section. The assumption about costs is not a decisive sticking point since it seems justifiable in empirical as well as normative terms. Public authorities no doubt are concerned about such things as the costs of equipment, training, and the time of personnel. But what about the assumption relating to the computation of benefits? Of course, it is possible to argue that public authorities have a "constitutional" mandate to keep social costs down or that the function of such authorities is the regulation of social costs.[14] But such arguments are all forms of functional teleology; they hardly constitute convincing explanations or predictions of the actual behavior of public authorities. To arrive at realistic conclusions requires some consideration of the motivations of a self-interested public authority.

Earlier work on institutional arrangements and bureaucratic behavior suggests a range of possibilities. Downs (1957, chap. 15) examines political parties whose principal aim is to win elections (or to capture the maximum number of votes in elections). Niskanen (1971) focuses on bureaus or agencies conceptualized as budget maximizers. Tullock (1965) assesses the behavior of bureaucrats on the assumption that individual bureaucrats seek to rise within their organizations as rapidly as possible. And Frohlich, Oppenheimer, and Young (1971) consider the choices of political leaders who attempt to maximize the *present* value of the income to be derived from occupying leadership roles.[15] However, none of these conceptions seems fully applicable to the behavior of the public authorities with which I am concerned. I believe that the most fruitful approach for purposes of empirical analysis is to assume that public authorities seek to maximize the probability of staying in power within viable social systems. That is, the self-interested public authority will be concerned both to prevent the collapse of the social system within which it operates and to ensure its own place in the system on a continuing basis. Such considerations will guide the public authority in all its activities, including those relating to compliance.

What are the implications of this assumption for the investment decisions of public authorities in the realm of compliance? Logically, there are three distinct possibilities. First, public authorities may find it in their

---

[14] For a concrete example of this sort of reasoning see Scott (1973, p. 54).

[15] For a more extensive discussion of the goals of political leaders see Frohlich and Oppenheimer (1978, chap. 4).

interest to minimize what I have been calling total costs in this chapter. Second, they may want to invest more in compliance mechanisms than suggested by the normative goal of minimizing total costs. Finally, such authorities may find it in their interests to invest less in compliance than required by the goal of minimizing total costs. In the following paragraphs, I want to comment briefly on each of these possibilities.

As I have said, public authorities will be interested in retaining power within viable social systems. But the probability of achieving this goal may well vary inversely with the level of social costs. The sources of this inverse correlation are not difficult to locate. Increases in violations and, therefore, social costs mean decreases in the prevailing quality of life in the system, including in extreme cases increases in the probability of systemic collapse. Should the social system itself collapse, the system's public authority would obviously be eliminated along with it. Further, reductions in the quality of life can only have a negative impact on the position of the public authority in the social system. Reductions in the quality of life ordinarily generate greater resentment and resistance than the perpetuation of long-standing conditions leading to a poor quality of life. Accordingly, the public authority of a social system is apt to have a definite interest in the reduction of social costs. And this concern will stem directly from the self-interest of the public authority rather than from any form of functional teleology.[16]

However, this argument hardly seems sufficient to cover the behavior of all public authorities under all circumstances. Consider, then, the second case referred to above. What would motivate a public authority to invest in compliance mechanisms beyond the point where total costs are minimized?[17] Put another way, what individuals or interest groups would benefit from the investment of resources in compliance beyond the point of TC_{min} and how much influence do these actors have on the choices of the public authority? Satisfactory conclusions concerning this question must of course await empirical studies in real-world situations. But it does not require a Marxist world view to realize that there will be cases in which some powerful members of a social system will reap large benefits from increased expenditures on compliance mechanisms, while the majority of members are injured only a little by such expenditures or are in no position to do anything about these injuries.[18] I suspect this is particularly

[16] This phenomenon might be regarded as somewhat analogous to the operation of the unseen hand in classical economics. For a more general exploration of this analogy consult McKean (1965).

[17] Recall that what I have called "social costs" are not costs to the public authority in any direct sense. To the extent that public authorities work to reduce social costs they will do so because it contributes to their chances of staying in power. Therefore, whenever public authorities find themselves in relatively secure positions, they can be expected to give weight to factors other than social costs (and compliance costs) in making decisions about the investment of resources in compliance mechanisms.

[18] The Marxian perspective suggests that those who own or control the means of production in a social system will benefit from precisely this sort of situation.

common in social systems organized along authoritarian or corporatist lines, but it is by no means impossible in systems that conform more closely to the basic tenets of democracy.[19]

Perhaps even more common are situations in which public authorities fail to invest as much in compliance mechanisms as would be required in order to minimize total costs. It is easy to see why this will be a frequent occurrence when public authorities are organized on a highly decentralized basis. This is simply a special case of the well-known problem of under-investment in collective goods (Olson, 1965 and Buchanan, 1968). That is, compliance mechanisms will typically exhibit the characteristics of collective goods from the perspective of the component parts of the public authority and each of these component parts may well experience the classic "free rider" tendencies.

When public authorities are organized on a more centralized basis (for example, systems in which formal institutions of government are present), it is not hard to find reasons for self-interested authorities to invest less in compliance mechanisms than would be required to minimize total costs. Two sets of conditions seem particularly noteworthy in this connection. In some situations, there will be subjects who wish to violate important behavioral prescriptions and who are powerful enough to affect significantly the fate of the relevant public authority itself. This is apt to lead to *pro forma* efforts on the part of the authority to achieve compliance coupled with a tacit acceptance of noncompliant behavior by the powerful subjects in question. The histories of many of the regulatory agencies in the United States, for example, are full of situations of this type. At the same time, there will be cases in which public authorities find it possible to extract resources from a body of constituents on a continuing basis without engaging in vigorous efforts to supply the collective good of compliance. To the extent that this is the case, the self-interested public authority will not be impelled to worry about the reduction of social costs. There is of course a need for systematic empirical research in this area, but I have no doubt that such situations occur frequently in the real world (Frohlich, Oppenheimer, and Young, 1971, pp. 62–65).

The conclusions suggested by this discussion are straightforward. It would be erroneous to suppose that self-interested public authorities will have no interest at all in the reduction of social costs. There will almost certainly be cases in which the normative model of the preceding section represents a reasonable approximation of real-world conditions. But it is extraordinarily naive to assume that public authorities will typically attempt to invest in compliance mechanisms in such a way as to minimize total costs.

---

[19] This may occur in cases where there are small minorities with intense preferences about various issues coupled with large majorities with much weaker preferences.

HOW TO INVEST IN COMPLIANCE MECHANISMS

In addition to making decisions concerning how much to invest in compliance mechanisms overall, public authorities will have to decide how to apportion these resources among the various feasible types of such mechanisms. Investing in compliance is not like investing in units of a more or less uniform good. There are many types of compliance mechanisms, and it is unlikely that they will all be equally effective when applied to concrete problems of compliance.

The effectiveness of any given technique for the achievement of compliance will be a function of such things as: (1) the nature of the behavioral prescription(s) in question, (2) the extent to which the relevant activity is highly iterative, (3) the size of the subject group, (4) the behavioral attributes of individual subjects, (5) the nature of the culture prevailing in the social system, and (6) the availability of relevant technologies. It follows that the investment of resources in compliance mechanisms is generally not a simple matter of making selections from some preexisting list of available mechanisms. Instead, investment decisions will require efforts to work out coordinated programs of mechanisms based on a careful analysis of the characteristics of the situation at hand.

In formulating compliance programs, public authorities will be guided by the criterion of efficiency. That is, they will seek to achieve the maximum amount of compliance for each unit of resources expended, given the specific characteristics of the relevant compliance problem. Note, however, that several complicating factors will impede these efforts in most real-world situations. First, the production functions associated with compliance mechanisms are likely to vary substantially, even in the context of the same compliance problem. The implications of this are portrayed in figure 10. Suppose these functions represent the expected productivity of three compliance mechanisms that could be utilized to deal with a given problem of compliance. For expenditures of resources on compliance below the level of x_1, mechanism 3 would be the most efficient. For levels of expenditure ranging from x_1 to x_2, on the other hand, mechanism 1 would produce the most efficient results. And for levels of expenditure exceeding x_2, the increasing marginal returns associated with mechanism 2 would yield the most efficient results. A second complication is that the exact shape of the production function for any given compliance mechanism will not be invariant across all problems of compliance. That is, the productivity of a particular mechanism will typically be affected by the specific characteristics of the compliance problem at hand. Therefore, it is not enough to identify the production functions for various compliance mechanisms once and for all. These functions must be recomputed in the light of the specific characteristics of each new problem of compliance. Third, though there may be simple cases in which the use of a single compliance mechanism will constitute an efficient program, the achieve-

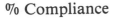

% Compliance

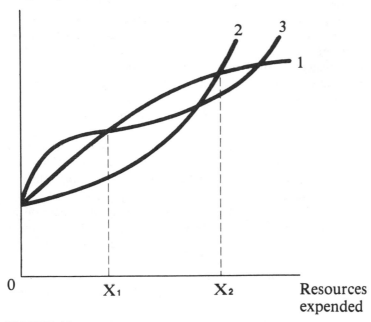

FIGURE 10

ment of efficiency will require the utilization of a mix of several compliance mechanisms in many concrete cases. Here it becomes necessary to decide how to apportion available resources among the various mechanisms included in the mix as well as to think about coordinating the mechanisms employed.

From what I have said in the preceding paragraphs it follows that the choice of compliance mechanisms will constitute an important decision variable for public authorities. The selection of such mechanisms will substantially affect the results flowing from the introduction of any given behavioral prescription. Moreover, rational decision makers will take into account expectations concerning problems of compliance in the initial formulation of the prescriptions. They will generally attempt to avoid prescriptions that would be difficult to enforce. All this suggests that decision makers acting for public authorities will devote considerable energy to the selection of compliance mechanisms for specific situations.[20] And they will frequently find it worthwhile to allocate resources to research and development relating to compliance mechanisms. Such research can never be definitive or exhaustive since the development of compliance mecha-

[20] It also suggests that bureaucratic politics will play a major role in compliance investment decisions. For an extensive examination of bureaucratic politics see Allison (1971).

nisms is essentially a matter of social invention, and new compliance problems arise continuously in most social systems. Nevertheless, I would expect to observe extensive research and development in this realm in many social systems, especially those characterized by rapid social change.

It is obviously impossible to assemble anything resembling a complete inventory of compliance mechanisms, let alone to rank them in terms of efficiency or productivity. However, it is possible to assess a number of mechanisms that are widely employed in efforts to elicit compliance efficiently. Below are some brief descriptions of and comments on a few such mechanisms.

The burden of proof. Public authorities are sometimes able to achieve efficient results in the realm of compliance by arranging to place the burden of demonstrating compliance squarely on the individual subject. The idea here is to presume noncompliance on the part of the subject until he proves decisively that he has in fact complied with the prescription in question. The crucial advantage of such arrangements from the perspective of the public authority is that they greatly reduce the need for surveillance and information gathering in the interests of checking on compliance.[21] A classic illustration of this technique is the presumption that alleged criminals are guilty until proven innocent. But there are many other more mundane cases in which the technique can be employed. For example, it is possible to deny production licenses to factories unless they can prove conclusively that they are able and willing to comply with the relevant emission control standards. Requests for landing rights at airports can be rejected until the carrier in question proves that it is in compliance with various safety standards. And imports of items like automobiles can be barred until conclusive evidence is presented that they conform to the specifications of the recipient country.

The critical condition involved in all these cases is the existence of some effective means of blockage under the control of the public authority. That is, the public authority controls something that is valued by the relevant subjects, whether this is personal freedom for the alleged criminal or the right to engage in profitable production or distribution for the factory owner. The use of this mechanism may produce normatively distasteful results in some situations. Thus, the idea of regarding an individual as guilty until proven innocent violates many philosophical precepts that place a high value on the civil liberties of the individual. But this is not always the case: few will question the proposition that factory owners or managers will violate emission control standards with some frequency unless it is made costly for them to do so (Kapp, 1950).

Contingent rewards. Somewhat related to the preceding mechanism is the idea of inducing subjects to comply with various prescriptions by

---

[21] Note that this would minimize invasions of privacy on the part of public authorities as well as cutting down on operating costs.

making significant rewards contingent upon compliance. Phrased differently, the procedure here is to withhold something of value to the subject unless he complies with the relevant prescriptions. For example, universities typically withhold degrees from students pending compliance with the prescription that one must pay one's bills. Similarly, parents often resort to withholding allowances or desired privileges unless children perform the chores that have been assigned to them. And a classic example of the use of contingent rewards involves the idea that entry into heaven will be withheld from subjects unless they comply with various religious prescriptions relating to proper behavior or the performance of good works. All these cases hinge on the existence of something that can be withheld and that the subjects value more than they value the benefits associated with noncompliant behavior. Of course, the public authority must establish credible control over the supply of the reward in question. In effect, it must develop an effective exclusion mechanism which will permit the supply of the reward to subjects on an individual basis (Frohlich and Oppenheimer, 1971, chap. 5). This, no doubt, accounts for the extensive resources that have been expended throughout history by religious authorities on efforts to persuade subjects that they can actually control access to heaven. Moreover, this discussion suggests that it will be advantageous for public authorities to control a variety of rewards. This will make it possible to elicit compliant behavior from large groups of subjects, even assuming significant variations with respect to their value systems.

Add ons. There are cases in which it is possible to link compliance with a behavioral prescription to some other action that members of the relevant subject group are almost certain to take. The idea here is to fashion an inseparable bond between the compliant behavior in question and the other action, so that, if an individual engages in the action, he will automatically comply with the behavioral prescription at the same time. Perhaps the classic illustrations of this mechanism occur in the realm of taxes. Value added taxes and sales taxes take this form, since it is necessary to pay the taxes in order to purchase the good in question. Similarly, gasoline taxes and luxury taxes on items like alcohol and perfume are typically levied in such a way as to make use of this compliance mechanism. It is of course clear that the critical condition for the use of this mechanism is the existence of some other action to which the relevant problem of compliance can be linked, but there are other important conditions as well. First, the link between the act of compliance and the other action must be made as firm as possible. This is why authorities often try to hide value added taxes or sales taxes by encouraging sellers to quote only the total price of various goods. Second, it helps if demand for the basic items is highly price inelastic so that authorities can levy high taxes without inducing subjects simply to refrain from purchasing the items altogether. This is undoubtedly a key factor in the great success of gasoline taxes in highly modernized societies.

Indirect compliance. Another mechanism that is highly successful in some situations involves depriving the subject of any choice in compliance. Here some other actor becomes responsible for ensuring compliance by primary actors. This will create another class of subjects and may produce a new range of compliance problems, but these problems are apt to turn out to be much easier to manage effectively than those involved in eliciting compliant behavior from the primary subjects. The classic example of the use of this mechanism is the system of withholding income taxes from salaries. Under this arrangement, employers are required to deduct income tax from the salary of each employee during each pay period. And the employee, who is the primary subject of the tax laws, no longer has any choice concerning whether or not he will pay his income tax. There are, however, other situations in which mechanisms of this type are utilized. Thus, banks often demand the authority to deduct mortgage payments directly from an individual's account without any specific action by the individual. A particularly attractive feature of this arrangement is that there is no intermediate party between the primary subject and the ultimate recipient of the payments (that is, the bank). Governments also frequently seek to make use of such arrangements by requiring banks to deduct property taxes as well as mortgage payments from the individuals' accounts. An obvious condition for the use of this mechanism is the existence of something of value to primary subjects (for example, salaries) which is under the control of some other actor. In addition, the public authority must be able to ensure compliance on the part of the intermediate actor to make this mechanism attractive. Little would be gained by the government if employers failed to transmit taxes withheld from the salaries of employees to the treasury. But it is typically cheaper for a government to obtain compliance in this area from a small number of employers than from a very large number of taxpayers.[22]

Isolation. Public authorities will often find it advantageous to isolate, at least partially, individuals from other members of their group. The basic reasons are to control the information available to those in the process of making decisions about compliance and to prevent coordination among those who may be contemplating noncompliant behavior. In this way, the public authority can reduce the subject's sense of efficacy as a potential violator and emphasize its own image as a prosecutor of those who fail to comply with behavioral prescriptions. There are numerous examples of the use of this mechanism, though many of them have distasteful normative implications. Thus, a public authority can attempt to prohibit individuals

---

[22] Paradoxically, it may benefit a group to be large and unorganized when the objective is to resist pressures for compliance rather than to demand some positive action. This phenomenon is the exact opposite of the frequently noted problems faced by large groups with respect to the supply of collective goods. See also Olson (1965) and Randall (1974).

from attending meetings or congregating in public places in order to discourage the occurrence of coordinated violations. It can endeavor to manipulate information about such matters as the level of tax evasion in the social system or the proportion of various types of crimes that ultimately go unpunished. And it can resort to censorship to prevent subjects from obtaining new ideas about how to violate behavioral prescriptions with impunity. Mechanisms of this kind are in fact employed regularly by authoritarian regimes anxious to control the behavior of large groups of subjects, whether or not the subjects acknowledge the legitimacy of any set of behavioral prescriptions. But the use of such mechanisms seems somewhat paradoxical in situations in which the great majority of subjects are perfectly willing to acknowledge the legitimacy of the behavioral prescriptions in question. Acceptance of such mechanisms by subjects would amount to their agreement to the use of indiscriminate coercion to ensure compliance with behavioral prescriptions that are in fact widely acknowledged as legitimate. That is, the sanctions associated with such mechanisms affect all members of the subject group regardless of whether they belong to the subset of current or prospective violators. This characteristic undoubtedly lies at the heart of the widespread tendency to reject the use of such mechanisms on normative grounds, despite the fact that they are apt to be efficient means of eliciting compliance in some situations.[23]

Internal guarantees.   Some compliance mechanisms are particularly suitable for use in situations in which there is no centralized public authority vested with the task of eliciting compliance with behavioral prescriptions. Consider the situation in which various actors are concerned about the ultimate implementation of the terms of an agreement or treaty. One common device used to cope with these problems is for one or more of the parties to offer some type of guarantee to the other or others. The crucial idea here is for the relevant parties deliberately to drive up the costs of noncompliant behavior on their own part. The effect of this is to reassure the other parties about the prospects of compliance on the part of the parties offering the guarantees (Schelling, 1960, chap. 2). In fact, the use of guarantees is relatively common in such situations. So, for example, recipients of loans frequently put up some form of collateral as a guarantee of repayment. Occupants of houses and apartments typically make a deposit whose purpose is to serve as a guarantee that they will ultimately leave the house or apartment in good condition. And the use of hostages constitutes a classic form of guarantee in intergroup and international affairs. For this mechanism to come into play, one or more of the relevant parties must be sufficiently anxious to reach an agreement to be willing to offer guarantees of some sort. Moreover, the parties must be in possession of something

---

[23] In the United States, for example, such mechanisms would almost invariably violate various provisions of the Bill of Rights as well as recent legislation dealing with the freedom of information.

of value that can serve as a guarantee. This is not a trivial condition; poor people are frequently barred from participating in agreements due to their lack of resources to put up as guarantees. Beyond this, the use of guarantees sometimes requires the existence of an impartial third party to hold the guarantee during the course of the agreement. This is particularly likely to be the case when the guarantees in question are unilateral rather than reciprocal.[24]

External guarantors. Another mechanism that can be used in situations of the type described in the preceding paragraph involves the introduction of external guarantors. In the event that internal guarantees are infeasible or too costly, it is possible to conduct a search for one or more outside actors to serve as guarantors of the compliant behavior of the primary parties to an agreement or a treaty. In effect, the external guarantor agrees either to compel the primary parties to conform to the terms of their agreement or to assume the obligations of the relevant primary parties in the event of violations. In fact, the use of this mechanism is relatively widespread. For example, cosigners of bank loans are actually external guarantors, and similar arrangements are often used to ensure the payment of telephone bills. Contracts for the rental of apartments sometimes require the leasee to locate an external actor to guarantee that he will pay all the specified bills and ultimately return the apartment in good condition. And the use of external guarantors is a well-known device in connection with international treaties relating to such things as neutralization arrangements and peace settlements.[25] Nevertheless, the conditions for the successful use of this mechanism are relatively stringent. It is necessary to find one or more outside actors who are both able and willing to serve as guarantors, and this may be a difficult condition to fulfill since the role of external guarantor will frequently be a relatively unattractive one. Then, it is necessary for the primary parties to have confidence that the external guarantor will actually carry out its duties under the terms of the agreement.[26] And this may require some method of resolving ambiguous cases or settling disputes, since there are apt to be many situations in which the extent of noncompliance on the part of the primary parties is unclear or the actions expected on the part of the guarantor are ambiguous. Under the circumstances, the use of external guarantors can hardly be regarded as an all-purpose method of coping with compliance problems in decentralized social systems.

[24] The absence of such impartial third parties is a key issue in the growing opposition of tenants to the traditional forms of security deposits.

[25] For an extensive discussion of guarantees in connection with neutralization arrangements see Black and coauthors (1968).

[26] It is not satisfactory simply to assume that external guarantors will behave in accordance with the terms of the relevant agreements. This is just as much a form of functional teleology as the assumption that public authorities will always seek to minimize social costs.

CHAPTER 8

Externalities of compliance mechanisms

There is good reason to doubt whether public authorities will always deal vigorously with problems of compliance. Chapter 3 explores in some depth the sources of this tendency with respect to highly decentralized social systems, such as the international system. But the same tendency will often emerge in more centralized social systems as well. Public authorities may reject the proposition that there is a close link between the level of social costs and their ability to remain in power. Or they may be unaware of the exact nature of this relationship. Further, public authorities will always feel the press of demands for resources from other quarters. Consequently, a certain lack of interest in problems of compliance and a tendency toward underinvestment in compliance mechanisms are apt to be common phenomena in social systems.

There is, however, another range of problems associated with the development and operation of compliance mechanisms which require more detailed treatment in a general theory of compliance. In their efforts to obtain compliance with various behavioral prescriptions, public authorities will often set up compliance mechanisms that produce unintended side effects or by-products seriously affecting the welfare of subjects. For example, the use of certain techniques of eliciting information will lead inadvertently to invasions of the privacy of many subjects, and efforts to prevent collusion among potential violators will often yield policies that amount to *de facto* censorship. Side effects of this kind are apt to become particularly prominent when public authorities find themselves under great pressure to achieve compliance efficiently, cutting corners in this area in order to devote more resources to other pressing problems. My objective in this final chapter, then, is to explore the nature of these unintended side effects and to evaluate various methods of regulating them.

THE NATURE OF THE PROBLEM

As I have presented it, the problem to be considered in this chapter is essentially a matter of "externalities." In the classic formulation of Pigou, externalities arise whenever ". . . one person A, in the course of rendering some service, for which payment is made, to a second person B, incidentally also renders services or disservices to other persons (not producers of like services), of such a sort that payment cannot be exacted from the benefitted parties or compensation enforced on behalf of the injured parties" (Pigou, 1932, p. 183). More generally, we can say that externalities are present whenever a subject attempts to achieve a specified objective efficiently without taking into account (or being forced to take into account) various inadvertent by-products of its activities affecting the welfare of others.[1] Classic illustrations of this phenomenon include such things as the smoke emitted into the atmosphere by industrial chimneys, the exhaust fumes from automobiles and commercial aircraft, and the noise generated by apartment dwellers who play their stereo systems late at night (Kapp, 1950).

All situations involving externalities raise certain basic questions. When should conscious efforts be made to regulate or to eliminate them? It does not follow that all externalities should be eliminated. Nor is it self-evident that the sources of costly externalities should always compensate the victims (Coase, 1960). Next, what criteria should be used in choosing methods to regulate externalities? The most common criterion in this connection concerns efficiency in the allocation of resources, but it is by no means clear that this criterion should predominate over considerations of distributive justice. There is also the question of what forum should be employed and what actors should take the lead in this process. In the literature, this issue has devolved largely into a debate concerning the proper role of government in this process, but the question is intrinsically a much broader one than this (Head, 1974, pp. 184–213). Finally, what specific means or techniques should be introduced in efforts to regulate externalities? There is in fact a lively debate concerning the relative merits of various policy instruments involving bargaining, liability rules, compulsory regulations, tax or subsidy schemes, and so forth.

The literature on externalities deals almost exclusively with side effects arising from interdependencies between or among actors in the private sector. These externalities are typically conceptualized as market imperfections (Bator, 1958). Accordingly, their analysis constitutes a digression or a diversion from the principal concerns of microeconomics. Thus, we have classic examples like Pigou's case of the sparks from railway engines damaging neighboring woods and Coase's case in which straying animals belonging to a cattle raiser damage the crops of a nearby farmer

---

[1] The effect of this broader formulation is to extend the range of externalities beyond the realm of competitive market transactions.

(Pigou, 1932, p. 134 and Coase, 1960, part III). And it is a simple matter to multiply these examples many times over, since the interdependencies underlying these illustrations are both extensive and important in most social systems. This is particularly true of highly developed social systems (Kapp, 1950).

The problem of externalities I am concerned with in this chapter differs fundamentally from the problems emphasized in the literature. I am not primarily interested in spillovers occurring in the private sector and in the extent to which government can or should intervene to regulate them. Instead, the problem I want to pursue involves externalities arising out of the relationships between the public authority on the one hand and members of the subject group on the other. The public authority seeks to elicit compliance with behavioral prescriptions as efficiently as possible. In so doing, it develops and operates various institutional arrangements designed to influence the choices of subjects concerning compliance and violation. But these arrangements, established by the public authority for legitimate purposes, will frequently generate externalities that have a substantial impact on the welfare of subjects.

In principle, subjects may evaluate these externalities either positively or negatively, and may differ among themselves in their evaluations. In this exploratory discussion, I shall be concerned primarily with the negative externalities of compliance mechanisms. Empirically, I am convinced that negative externalities are predominant. While there may occasionally be positive side effects of compliance mechanisms, their negative byproducts in such realms as censorship, restrictions of civil liberties, and invasions of privacy are notorious. Moreover, I personally am concerned primarily about negative externalities on straightforward normative grounds. Though I am well aware of the importance of social costs arising from high levels of violations, I have a deep commitment to the goal of protecting the rights of individuals from serious erosion due to the operation of various compliance mechanisms. Therefore, the central concern of this chapter is the problem of limiting the harm done by the externalities of compliance mechanisms without producing severe losses of efficiency in the pursuit of compliance.

TRADE-OFFS

Though the temptation is clear, it is important to avoid thinking in purely dichotomous terms in connection with efforts to regulate the externalities of compliance mechanisms. The dichotomous perspective suggests that it is necessary to choose between the elimination of such externalities coupled with a severe loss of efficiency, on the one hand, and a high degree of efficiency accompanied by unusually severe externalities on the other. But this perspective poses the problem in its starkest form. In fact, it is generally possible to identify intermediate positions involving various trade-offs between efficiency and the magnitude of the harmful externalities flowing from the operation of compliance mechanisms.

It will help to think about these prospects more precisely if we examine them in graphical terms. Figure 11 outlines two possible relationships between the achievement of efficiency in the pursuit of compliance and the protection of individual privacy. The X axis in these graphs is a measure of privacy, while the Y axis represents the variable labeled efficiency. It is, of course, difficult to calibrate the axes of these graphs with precision, but it is not difficult to think in general terms about increases or decreases in both efficiency and privacy. The curves in the two graphs can be interpreted as transformation functions (Zeckhauser and Shaefer, 1968, pp. 30–36). They map the rate at which privacy must be sacrificed to obtain efficiency and vice versa. In part a of the figure, the marginal rate of substitution is such that there are decreasing returns in terms of efficiency for sacrifices of privacy. By contrast, part b portrays the opposite relationship between efficiency and privacy. It is also possible to interpret the area under the curve in each graph as a production possibility set. That is, every point in this space represents a feasible combination of efficiency and privacy in the social system in question. Both the locus and the shapes of the curves are essentially matters of physical and social technology. Accordingly, it is reasonable to assume that there will be considerable variation among social systems with respect to these matters. In fact, I can see no *a priori* basis for concluding that cases resembling part a are more prevalent in the real world than cases resembling part b, or vice versa. The fact that transformation functions are generally thought to exhibit the shape illustrated in part a in microeconomics does not strike me as conclusive evidence that the same situation will obtain for trade-offs between efficiency and the externalities of compliance mechanisms. It seems clear that this subject requires systematic empirical investigation in efforts to make applications to real-world situations.

What are the policy implications of this perspective on the externalities of compliance mechanisms? To begin with, there is no doubt that compliance mechanisms yielding Pareto inferior outcomes should be abandoned. Consider, for example, a set of institutional arrangements producing results identified by the point v in figure 11a. Here there is ample room for Pareto optimal moves. That is, an outcome falling anywhere on the segment of the transformation function labeled rs would be both feasible and preferred by everyone to the outcome at point v. In the absence of prohibitive transactions costs, therefore, it is reasonable to expect that the institutional arrangements leading to the outcome at point v will be abandoned and that the welfare of all the relevant parties will improve.

But what alternative institutional arrangements should be chosen? Or, to put it another way, where on the segment of the transformation function

Efficiency

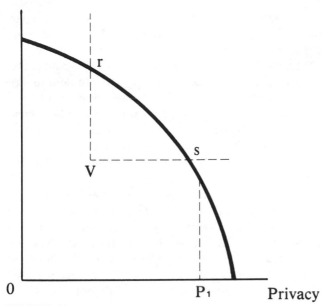

FIGURE 11a

Efficiency

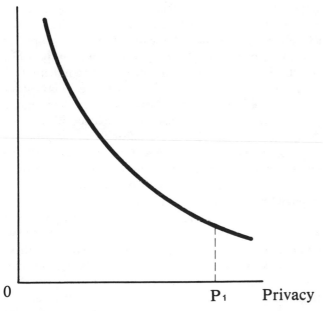

FIGURE 11b

139

labeled rs should the final outcome lie? This situation yields a classic bargaining problem (Young, 1975). Everyone would prefer any point on rs to the outcome labeled v, but there will be conflicts of interest concerning the exact point on rs to select. No doubt, the public authority would prefer an outcome as close to r as possible. This would serve to promote its primary goal of efficiency. Members of the subject group, by contrast, may exhibit a range of preferences. Many will wish to maximize the achievement of privacy (that is, they will advocate an outcome as close to s as possible), but others will remember the link between efficiency and reduced social costs and advocate the selection of an outcome somewhere between r and s. Under the circumstances, the actual outcome in each case will flow from some sort of bargaining process. For reasons that I will explain later in this chapter, I believe that the bargaining strength of public authorities in these situations will be considerably greater than the strength of members of the subject group. This implies that outcomes will typically fall closer to the point labeled r in my illustration than to the point labeled s. Are such outcomes normatively desirable? Given my personal normative preferences, I would say no, though I have little doubt that they are likely to occur.

There are also important policy implications associated with the shapes of the curves in figure 11. Imagine that we begin at the point labeled P_1 in either of the cases. In case 11a, it is possible to achieve large and striking gains in efficiency by making relatively small sacrifices of privacy. Here many subjects may even place a higher value on the increases in efficiency (which can be translated into reduced social costs) than on the losses in privacy. Such subjects will actually be willing to initiate proposals for changes along these lines. In case 11b, the opposite situation prevails. Starting from point P_1, striking gains in efficiency will require much larger sacrifices in terms of privacy. Here there are likely to be many fewer subjects who will be untroubled about the losses of privacy they would have to accept in order substantially to increase the efficiency with which the public authority could pursue compliance. It follows from this line of argument that case 11a offers much more scope than case 11b for the avoidance of both severe conflict between the public authority and groups of subjects and serious repression of the basic rights of the subjects.

What other policy guidelines are relevant to this discussion of tradeoffs? The arguments I have advanced so far are not sufficient to produce a recommended solution for most real-world cases. It is very well to suggest such things as the abandonment of Pareto inferior arrangements, but these proposals do nothing to pinpoint preferred points along the transformation functions. At best, they indicate things to avoid rather than providing persuasive arguments in favor of specific outcomes. The problem here is that the analysis I have advanced in the preceding paragraphs ultimately emerges as a special case of modern welfare economics (Rothenberg,

1961). From the perspective of policy implications, it exhibits all the drawbacks of welfare economics (Head, 1974, pp. 3–49). Nevertheless, this discussion clearly indicates that any major advances in the realm of welfare economics should also shed light on the problems associated with efforts to regulate the externalities of compliance mechanisms.

CONTROL TECHNIQUES

Suppose it is deemed desirable to regulate or to eliminate some particular externality arising from the operation of a compliance mechanism. How is it possible to accomplish this objective? The usual prescriptions flowing from the Coasean and Pigovian traditions will not be of much help.[2] Nor am I especially optimistic about the prospects of developing other control techniques that are both highly effective and relatively simple to introduce. Nevertheless, I shall conclude this chapter with an examination of what I believe to be the major options.

The Coasean tradition emphasizes reliance on private interactions between the relevant parties in efforts to regulate externalities (Coase, 1960 and Buchanan, 1962). The underlying presumptions of this approach are that the parties will be able to bargain with each other effectively and that the achievement of efficiency in the allocation of resources is the paramount concern. Where compliance mechanisms are concerned, however, there are serious problems with this approach. To begin with, real-world situations here typically violate several of the major Coasean assumptions. It is not reasonable to expect anything approaching perfectly competitive markets for the goods or factors of production involved. On the contrary, there will generally be no markets at all for these goods. Similarly, the assumption of perfect information is particularly inappropriate. While public authorities may be relatively well informed about the issues at stake, it must be expected that individual subjects will usually be poorly informed. Moreover, the transactions costs associated with efforts to regulate the externalities of compliance mechanisms will often be high. There are no institutional arrangements in this realm which can match the smooth workings of a competitive market.

There are also compelling reasons to expect that the Coasean approach will lead to severe distributive injustices. In essence, the problem here stems from the weakness of groups of subjects relative to the public authority. Subjects will typically be dispersed and without access to an effective agent or leader, while the public authority can operate as a unified entity. The public authority will have distinct advantages in the realm of information; it will often be able to manipulate the information available to individual subjects about the principal issues at stake. And the public authority will be able to command far more extensive material re-

---

[2] For a survey of the relevant literature see Mishan (1971).

sources than the individual subjects. Under the circumstances, it is to be expected that the public authority will be the dominant party in negotiations relating to the regulation of the externalities of compliance mechanisms (Randall, 1974). Therefore, reliance on the Coasean approach in this realm is apt to yield results that are neither efficient in allocative terms nor just in distributive terms.

The Pigovian approach focuses on administrative intervention employing tax or subsidy schemes, liability rules, or even outright prohibitions, and there are those who maintain that it constitutes the preferred way to cope with externalities arising in the private sector (Staaf and Tannian, 1973, and Davis and Kamien, 1969). However, I am convinced that this approach is no more likely than the Coasean approach to yield desirable results with respect to efforts to regulate the externalities of compliance mechanisms. In the first instance, most of the standard criticisms of this approach are just as relevant when it is applied to the problems under consideration here as when it is applied to externalities arising in the private sector (Head, 1974, pp. 199–210). In the absence of anything resembling market transactions, it is difficult (if not impossible) to make meaningful judgments concerning the value systems or preferences of the relevant actors. Outcomes are apt to reflect the biases of administrative officials more than the true preferences of the affected parties. Moreover, the inability of administrative measures to discriminate effectively among individual cases is just as pertinent here as it is in other realms. Administrative regulations ordinarily take the form of general prescriptions while it would be desirable to deal with actual externalities on a case-by-case basis to achieve both allocative efficiency and distributive justice.

Beyond this, however, there is a more fundamental problem with the Pigovian approach as a response to the externalities of compliance mechanisms. The situation here differs fundamentally from the traditional case of externalities occurring in the private sector. There it is at least plausible to propose that the government serve as a more or less impartial regulator.[3] In the case at hand, however, the government (or whatever other public authority is involved) will itself be one of the affected parties. Of course, it may not be entirely unreasonable to look to public authorities to play some role in regulating the externalities of compliance mechanisms. There are, for example, situations in which a government is composed of many agencies and in which there are elaborate arrangements for some of these agencies to play a role in regulating the behavior of others. Similarly, it is easy to identify situations in which it is possible to appeal to a higher public authority against the actions of some lower public authority. If I am sufficiently displeased with the actions of an official of my local school board, for example, I can bring a suit against that official in some appro-

[3] Even in these cases, it is by no means self-evident that the government will be motivated to play the role of impartial regulator (Downs, 1957, pp. 279–294).

priate court. Nevertheless, I do not think it is reasonable to rely very heavily on these prospects. Fundamentally, there is no escaping the fact that the Pigovian approach raises the classic *quis custodiet* issue when it is applied to the regulation of the externalities of compliance mechanisms.

What, then, is to be done about the regulation of this type of externality? As I have already suggested, I do not think there is an ideal solution to this problem. However, I do want to examine two responses that may offer some hope. To begin with, there is the idea of encouraging effective organization on the part of various subject groups. The presumption underlying this approach is that developments along these lines would have the effect of increasing the bargaining strength of subjects in their interactions with public authorities. This would serve both to compel public authorities to negotiate about the regulation of the externalities and to improve the ultimate outcomes for the affected subjects when such negotiations do take place.

There are, however, serious problems with this approach. The benefits flowing from such organization would often take the form of collective goods (Olson, 1965 and Frohlich and Oppenheimer, 1971, chap. 2). Therefore, individual subjects would experience free-rider incentives with respect to organizing along these lines, and there would be a general tendency toward underinvestment in these organizations (Olson, 1965). Moreover, even when free-rider tendencies can be overcome through the development of effective exclusion mechanisms, the transactions costs of efforts to organize are still apt to be high. There will typically be extensive costs associated with such things as the dissemination of the relevant information, the introduction of coordination mechanisms, and the development of effective leadership. These costs will of course rise as a function of the extent to which the public authority actively opposes the organization of subjects. And opposition of this type must be expected to occur frequently since public authorities will ordinarily face less favorable production functions in the realm of compliance when subjects are organized than when they are unorganized.

What can we conclude from this discussion? In general, the prospects for effective organization among subjects will be greatest when the subject group is small and the public authority is weak. Small groups are sometimes able to overcome the problem of underinvestment in collective goods through internal bargaining processes (Olson, 1965, pp. 43–52 and Young, 1975). And the transactions costs associated with organization of this type will ordinarily be substantially lower in the face of a weak public authority. With respect to large groups of subjects, on the other hand, the prospects do not seem promising. It may sometimes be reasonable to hope for the supply of protection from the externalities of compliance mechanisms as an Olsonian by-product (Olson, 1965, chap. 6). That is, groups which organize for other purposes may sometimes supply protection from certain negative externalities of compliance mechanisms as a by-product of their major activities. But I do not think that it is realistic to rely heavily on this prospect. Therefore, I conclude that encouraging the organization of subject groups does not constitute a generally satisfactory approach to the regulation of the externalities of compliance mechanisms.

The second response that strikes me as interesting centers on efforts to develop what I shall call "safeguards." A safeguard is an institutionalized arrangement designed explicitly to protect subjects from the harmful externalities of compliance mechanisms without vitiating the efforts of public authorities to achieve efficiency. Are effective safeguards of this type feasible? I am not overly optimistic about the prospects for such safeguards, but there are a number of factors about them that deserve some consideration at this point.

I think it is useful to distinguish between substantive safeguards and procedural safeguards. Substantive safeguards amount to what are called liability rules in the literature on externalities (Randall, 1974 and Calabresi, 1972). That is, they are systems of rights and rules spelling out who is responsible for the harmful effects arising from specified externalities. There are in fact two ways of thinking about these safeguards. As rules outlining prescribed behavior under specified conditions, they are a type of behavioral prescription, and they raise questions about compliance just like any other prescriptions. On the other hand, these safeguards take the form of formulas spelling out the compensation due to the victims of negative externalities under stated conditions. In this sense, such safeguards can be interpreted as devices to offset the bargaining weakness of subjects vis-à-vis public authorities. Substantive safeguards can take various forms, and in many social systems they are not highly developed. Nevertheless, I think it is reasonable to look upon the kinds of provisions often incorporated in "bills of rights" as at least rudimentary safeguards of this type.

Procedural safeguards, by contrast, are institutionalized devices designed not to specify the rights of subjects but rather to ensure that these rights are not suppressed without due process. It is easy to illustrate the nature of these devices from the practice of democratic governments. Thus, subjects may be allowed to bring suit against the government (or its agents) if they believe that their rights are being infringed. The presumption of innocence until proven guilty in criminal cases is a procedural safeguard to ensure that the rights of individuals are not inadvertently suppressed. And the use of ombudsmen is quite common in some systems as a device through which subjects can gain a hearing for their complaints. It should be emphasized that these procedural devices are not intended only to regulate the externalities of compliance mechanisms. In fact, it may seem highly desirable to introduce them even if there is no problem of externalities (Reich, 1964). Nevertheless, it is not uncommon for such devices to serve as procedural safeguards in connection with the negative externalities of compliance mechanisms.

In addition to the distinction concerning types of safeguards, there is the issue of how such safeguards can be introduced in social systems. It seems to me that this issue must be subdivided into two separate cases. In the first instance, there is what might be called the constitutional case. Thus, new social structures are sometimes established quite deliberately and their institutional arrangements may be outlined more or less explicitly in formal or informal constitutions (Dahl, 1956 and Buchanan and Tullock, 1962). Admittedly, this is an uncommon occurrence at the rather grand level of whole polities, but some such process occurs quite regularly where lesser social structures are concerned. This is true, for example, of clubs, community organizations, business cooperatives, nature societies, and so forth. Here it seems to me that the introduction of the kinds of safeguards under discussion is a common occurrence. The exact content of these safeguards will ordinarily be the outcome of extensive bargaining among various interests.[4] And the inclusion of such safeguards in a formal or informal constitution certainly does not constitute a guarantee that they will be effective in practice. Nevertheless, I see no reason to be pessimistic about the introduction of safeguards in what I have called the constitutional case.

The other case involves the introduction of safeguards in an ongoing social system. The idea here is to graft various safeguards onto an existing set of institutional arrangements without restructuring the constitution of the system. In general, I regard this as a far more difficult and chancy enterprise than the creation of safeguards in the constitutional case. For one thing, ongoing systems are typically characterized by the presence of powerful vested interests and built-in obstacles to change. While everything is apt to be up for change in a constitutional convention, the intrinsic advantages lie with the forces opposed to change in an ongoing system. In addition, successful efforts to introduce safeguards of the type under discussion here in an ongoing system will almost always require the achievement of substantial organization among subjects. But this raises once again all the problems to which I referred earlier in this section. Accordingly, I am convinced that the introduction of safeguards in ongoing systems will always be an extremely difficult process and that real successes (in contrast to superficial institutional tinkering) will be few and far between.[5]

Finally, I will turn to the question of the effectiveness of safeguards. Imagine a social system in which there exists an extensive set of safeguards

[4] Contrast this with the perspective of Rawls (1971) who views constitution making as a consensual process.

[5] It is worth noting, however, that changes along these lines are sometimes achieved on a *de facto* basis through processes of constitutional interpretation.

designed to protect the subjects from the most severe effects of the negative externalities of compliance mechanisms. What reason is there to expect that these safeguards will actually operate effectively in practice? It seems to me that it is helpful to think of this issue as yet another problem of compliance.[6] Thus, it is quite possible to conceptualize such safeguards in terms of behavioral prescriptions relating to the actions of public authorities. In short, they specify things that public authorities are expected to do under some conditions and to refrain from doing under other conditions. Looked at in this way, the question of effectiveness becomes a matter of examining the incentive structures of public authorities.

There is a definite tendency to jump to rather pessimistic conclusions concerning this issue. What sorts of sanctions can be brought to bear on public authorities with regard to the use of safeguards? Cannot public authorities often disregard such safeguards with impunity and perhaps with enough manipulation of information to confuse many subjects about the extent to which they have in fact been ignored? (Frohlich, Oppenheimer, and Young, 1971, especially chap. 2). While such pessimistic arguments are undoubtedly applicable in some social systems, I do not believe they accurately reflect the position of all public authorities. In some cases, at least, there will be good reasons for public authorities to take these safeguards seriously. For example, if public authorities seek to remain in power, some will find it in their self-interest to abide by these safeguards because of the possibility of organized resistance or even revolt by subject groups, if the situation becomes too unpleasant.[7] Similarly, there will be some cases in which public authorities will in fact have to concern themselves with the prospect of sanctions in this context. This will be the case whenever there are higher or more powerful public authorities to whom appeals against the behavior of a particular public authority can be directed. We often ignore this prospect by focusing our attention on the highest or most inclusive level of government. But the fact is that most public authorities operate in an environment containing one or more higher public authorities which are capable, at least in principle, of bringing sanctions to bear on them. Beyond this, there is the phenomenon of political culture, which can be interpreted in this connection as a form of socialization. That is, there will be some social systems in which the individuals who operate the public authority grow up in an environment in which the idea of respect for institutionalized safeguards is inculcated as an important value. In such circumstances, adherence to these safeguards may become an article of faith or a habit (Chayes, 1972). I do not know how common this phenomenon is in fact, but it surely exists. There-

---

[6] Again, contrast this perspective with the views expressed in Rawls (1971, p. 351).

[7] Even Hobbes recognizes the possibility of revolt by subjects. Locke devotes considerable attention to identifying the conditions under which he regards revolt by subjects as legitimate.

fore, I do not think it would be accurate to conclude that the safeguards I have been discussing in this section are bound to be ineffective, even in situations where it proves impossible to introduce them explicitly (Schapera, 1967). I am under no illusion that such responses to the problem of the externalities of compliance mechanisms remotely resemble a panacea. But I do believe that responses along these lines are worthy of more detailed investigation with reference to the substantive characteristics of specific situations.

Bibliographical note

One of the great pleasures of writing about what I have called the problem of compliance is that it has given me an opportunity to read widely in a number of fields or disciplines. The problem of compliance arises in one form or another in most human endeavors. Whether the subjects are individuals or complex corporate entities, the extent to which they comply with behavioral prescriptions and the factors governing their actions in this area are matters of intense and continuing concern. At the same time, the problem of compliance has never emerged as a recognized field of enquiry in its own right. Rather, materials pertaining to this problem are scattered widely through a variety of differentiable fields. Any systematic consideration of compliance, therefore, can hardly proceed without taking account of the ways in which it has been approached in a number of separate disciplines.

The purpose of this bibliographical note is to convey some sense of the range of materials I found helpful in preparing this study. I shall make no effort to be exhaustive or to note every source I consulted in the course of my research. Instead, I shall single out the most important sources of ideas and place particular stress on what strike me as seminal books and articles. I shall also group these sources roughly into recognizable fields of enquiry to give some idea of the range of disciplines across which the problem of compliance is relevant.

1. *Political science.* One might surmise that students of politics would have devoted a great deal of attention to the problem of compliance; behavioral prescriptions (in such forms as laws, administrative rules, and political norms) are central political phenomena. Nevertheless, the literature on politics seems to me disappointing in this respect. While students

of politics have certainly described legislative processes and the problems of translating laws into practice, they have seldom focused on the interactions between subjects and public authorities regarding compliance.

All this is not to say that work in this field is of no interest at all for an examination of the problem. For example, I have profited greatly from the thoughts of political scientists on the themes of power and authority. There is much to be learned from a careful study of Lasswell and Kaplan (1950). Another far-reaching treatment of these phenomena which has stood up well over time is de Jouvenel (1963). The classic works of anarchism contain much thought-provoking material on the link between compliance and the phenomena of power and authority (Shatz, 1971). A considerably different perspective on these issues emerges from Dahl (1956). Similarly, I have found the thoughts of political philosophers on the theme of obligation and consent particularly pertinent to my thinking about compliance. Of special merit are the essays of Pitkin (1965 and 1966). The most helpful collection of materials in this area is Pennock and Chapman (1970). Additional thoughts of interest along these lines appear in Quinton (1967).

2. *Philosophy.* There are no doubt many branches of philosophy which bear in some way on the problem of compliance. In my own work, however, I have found two types of philosophical enquiries of special relevance. The first concerns the nature of rules and laws. Numerous observations on rules appear in Wittgenstein (1953). An excellent introduction to laws in the realm of scientific thinking is Hempel (1966). Rules of various types are treated in an interesting fashion in Lewis (1969). Essays in the contractarian tradition were also a rich vein of ideas for my examination of compliance. In addition to the classics in this area (for example, Hobbes, Locke, Rousseau, Hume), there is a recent literature of special interest. The most influential work of this sort is undoubtedly Rawls (1971). This study is critiqued in an illuminating way in Barry (1973). As an alternative to Rawls, Nozick (1974) is helpful.

3. *Law and legal philosophy.* The problem of compliance is deeply embedded in most forms of legal reasoning. Work in this field ordinarily places primary emphasis on prescriptions in the form of laws and on enforcement as a basis of compliance. But issues relating to compliance are probably nearer the surface in legal writings than in the works of any other discipline. An examination of various traditions of legal thought, therefore, is essential for any systematic treatment of the problem of compliance.

In the realm of jurisprudence, I have found the continuing dialogue between H.L.A. Hart and Lon L. Fuller an extremely rich source of ideas for my reflections on compliance. The basic issues at stake are articulated in the so-called Hart-Fuller debate: Hart (1958) and Fuller (1958). Hart (1961) offers a fuller statement of the positivist viewpoint while Fuller

(1969) presents the modern natural law alternative in greater detail. A more general survey of modern jurisprudential perspectives is Goulding (1966). I have also discovered much of value for my contemplation of compliance in legal treatments of various concrete problems. The policy-oriented work of the "New Haven School" has taught me that it is often hazardous to think about compliance in simple dichotomous terms (Mc-Dougal and Associates, 1960). There are numerous implications for compliance in the changing conceptions of property described in Reich (1964). Taylor (1970) offers many insights concerning the general problem of compliance in the course of trying to think through the problem of war crimes. And a wealth of issues relating to compliance in highly decentralized sociopolitical systems, like the international system, are examined provocatively in Falk (1970).

4. *Economics.* The problem of compliance is often abstracted away in the behavioral postulates of mainstream neoclassical economics. Never-theless, the writings of economists have contributed greatly to the develop-ment of my thinking about compliance. Recent work on the economics of crime is of obvious relevance in this connection. The seminal work in this domain is Becker (1968). This line of thinking is extended in Stigler (1970), and several efforts have been made to make empirical applica-tions of these theoretical ideas in recent years (Tullock, 1974). The major components of this stream of work are brought together in Becker and Landes (1974). Some alternative perspectives emerge from Rottenberg (1973).

My own approach to the problem of compliance also owes much to the work of economists on various nonmarket phenomena such as externalities or social costs and property systems. The link between these phenomena and the central concerns of economics is articulated clearly in Bator (1958). The principal approaches to the treatment of externalities derive from Pigou (1932) on the one hand and Coase (1960) on the other. A good survey of the theoretical literature in this area is Staaf and Tannian (1973). The proposition that externalities or social costs are empirically pervasive is argued at length in Kapp (1950). Furubotn and Pejovich (1972) offer a good survey of recent work by economists on property rights.

5. *Public choice.* The new field of public choice (or nonmarket deci-sion making or modern political economy) reflects a growing interest in utilizing the formal, theoretical procedures of economics to generate an improved understanding of problems in the realm of politics or traditional political economy. So far, this work has traded heavily on the assumptions associated with neo-classical microeconomics (e.g. rationality, self-interest, expected-utility maximization), but there is no reason to regard this as a defining characteristic of public choice as a field of enquiry. A relatively comprehensive survey of this work is Riker and Ordeshook (1973). But see also Frohlich and Oppenheimer (1978).

I have been much involved with the development of this field in recent years, and my work on the problem of compliance reflects this involvement in numerous ways. Specifically, I have found several streams of work in the realm of public choice of particular help in my reflections on compliance. Theoretical arguments pertaining to collective action and the supply of collective or public goods constitute one such stream. The seminal work here is Olson (1965). Subsequent developments can be traced in Buchanan (1968) and Frohlich, Oppenheimer, and Young (1971). Studies of constitutional arrangements and ways of organizing public authorities have also been prominent in the field of public choice. Of particular relevance to my consideration of compliance are Buchanan and Tullock (1962), Taylor (1976), and Buchanan (1975). Works dealing with a variety of other public choice concerns have offered additional insights for my study of compliance. Schelling (1960) is an unusually imaginative analysis of bargaining, while Young (1975) surveys and critiques existing theoretical work on bargaining and negotiation. Much of interest concerning the problem of compliance in organizational settings is contained in Downs (1967) and Niskanen (1971). An examination of rules written explicitly from a public choice perspective is McKean (1974).

6. *Decision theory.*   Given my interpretation of compliance as a matter of choice, studies of decision processes have naturally played a central role in the development of the arguments set forth in this essay. Analyses of choice are incorporated in a number of disciplines, but it is increasingly meaningful to identify decision theory as a field of enquiry in its own right. The major streams of theoretical work falling under the heading of utility theory are represented in Page (1968). A survey encompassing behavioral as well as axiomatic treatments of decision processes is Edwards and Tversky (1967). Simon's (1959) effort to assess these several streams of decision theory remains illuminating even though it was published in 1959.

Decision theory as a field of enquiry divides into formal or axiomatic work on the one hand and experimental work on the other. For the study of compliance, the formal work associated with the theory of games has struck me as particularly helpful. Luce and Raiffa's (1957) survey, remains, in many ways, the most helpful general account. A variety of difficulties arising in efforts to apply game-theoretic perspectives to real-world situations are discussed in Rapoport (1964). On the experimental side, I have found work on human choices under conditions of conflict especially helpful (Rapoport and Chammah, 1965). Tversky and Kahneman (1974) open up another line of experimental work on decision processes which is distinctly relevant for efforts to understand compliance.

7. *Anthropology.*   Though anthropologists have seldom focused directly on the problem of compliance, I have profited greatly from their work in two areas. On the one hand, anthropological studies have increased my

awareness of cultural variations in attitudes and orientations toward compliance. At the same time, work of this sort has helped me to understand more fully the bases of compliance by exploring the behavior of subjects in highly decentralized social systems which do not have formalized institutions of government. Broadly based studies of primitive systems have proven particularly helpful in these realms. Of course, there is no substitute for a consideration of the classic work of Malinowski (1926). More recent works in this genre that have struck me as especially illuminating include: Mair (1962) and Schapera (1967). Anthropological studies of more specific topics have also helped me considerably in thinking through certain aspects of the problem of compliance. I have found much of value, for example, in the legal anthropology presented in Hoebel (1954). Similarly, I was fascinated by the treatment of social mores and pressures in Wylie (1974).

8. *Sociology.* Though I do not consider myself expert in the field of sociology, it is my impression that sociological literature is not particularly rich in insights for the examination of compliance. Perhaps this is attributable to the fact that sociologists have typically focused on human groups rather than on interactions between public authorities and individual subjects. Even so, I have derived some important insights for my study of compliance from sociological literature. Some of these insights stem from macrosociological works that deal with social structures treated as wholes. Not surprisingly, I have found much of interest along these lines in the writings of Max Weber—see Gerth and Mills (1958). Emmet (1972) contains numerous observations about rules from a sociological point of view. Levy (1972) presents an assessment of the prospects for contemporary social systems which has extensive implications for efforts to achieve compliance in the future. A number of works of microsociology have also helped me to work out my conception of the behavior of the individual subject in the realm of compliance. The March and Simon (1958) volume remains a helpful compendium of scientific hypotheses and propositions about human behavior in organized groups. A general discussion of sociological perspectives on crime and criminal behavior appears in Glasser (1972). The insights of Goffman are continually fascinating in efforts to think about the arational elements in human behavior. See, for example, Goffman (1971).

9. *Psychology and social psychology.* So far as I can tell, compliance as such has never emerged as a recognized topic for enquiry among psychologists and social psychologists. In fact, I have experienced some difficulty in communicating the essence of what I call the problem of compliance to colleagues in the field of psychology. This may be partly due to the fact that I place so much emphasis on choice in my own thinking about compliance. But it also seems to arise from the fact that compliance is not a recognized research topic among psychologists and social psychologists.

Research dealing with the theme of conformity appears to come as close to the problem of compliance as any work in psychology. There is a section on this topic in Cartwright and Zander (1968). More recent work on conformity is discussed in Kiesler and Kiesler (1969). I have found research on reciprocal relationships and the norm of reciprocity in social interactions particularly helpful in examining the bases of compliance (Gergen, 1969). Social psychological studies of small groups frequently offer comments on the reasons why individuals comply with (or fail to comply with) group rules and standards. In this connection, I have profited particularly from Thibaut and Kelley (1959). Another work in this area which is imaginative, though somewhat unsystematic, is Janis (1972). Beyond this, studies of socialization have obvious implications for the problem of compliance. In this area, I have benefited especially from Bronfenbrenner (1970).

10. *International relations and foreign policy.* The literature on international relations is largely an amalgam of ideas from a number of other disciplines. Accordingly, it is not easy to characterize it with any precision. Nor has compliance as such been a major focus of interest among students of international relations and foreign policy. Since I have a special interest in compliance in the international system, however, it is pertinent to identify the most relevant sources for a consideration of compliance at this level. Roughly speaking, these sources can be separated into general works on various aspects of international relations and more specific studies of sanctions or enforcement arrangements at the international level.

Recent thinking about the distinctive features of international society is reflected in Mendlovitz (1975), Keohane and Nye (1977), Bull (1977), and Young (1978). Helpful explorations of the external behavior of the individual actors in the international system include: Henkin (1968), Allison (1971), and Steinbruner (1974). Neustadt (1970) offers a rich descriptive account of the behavior of individual states when interacting with other clearly identified members of the international system. A sophisticated treatment of the role of force in international society appears in Schelling (1966). Problems of arms control and disarmament are illuminated in Schelling and Halperin (1961) as well as in the essays reprinted in York (1973). Factual information on armaments and arms control at the international level is readily available in the annual publication of the Stockholm International Peace Research Institute (SIPRI) entitled *World Armaments and Disarmament.*

In the realm of sanctions and enforcement arrangements, general accounts include Doxey (1971) and especially Reisman (1971). Compliance mechanisms relating to arms control arrangements are analyzed with particular insight in Chayes (1972) and explored at greater length in Falk and Barnet (1965). Similar phenomena outside the realm of peace and security are analyzed in Tauber (1969); Fisher (1971); Oliver (1971); and Burke, Legatski, and Woodhead (1975).

Reference list

Allison, Graham. 1971. *The Essence of Decision* (Boston, Little Brown).

Baldwin, David A. 1971. "The Power of Positive Sanctions," *World Politics,* vol. XXIV, pp. 19–38.

———. 1976. "Bargaining with Airline Hijackers," in I. William Zartman, ed. *The 50% Solution* (Garden City, Doubleday), pp. 404–429.

Barry, Brian. 1970. *Sociologists, Economists and Democracy* (London, Collier Macmillan).

———. 1973. *The Liberal Theory of Justice* (London, Oxford University Press).

Bator, Francis M. 1958. "The Anatomy of Market Failure," *Quarterly Journal of Economics,* vol. LXXII, pp. 351–379.

Becker, Gary S. 1968. "Crime and Punishment: An Economic Approach," *Journal of Political Economy,* vol. 76, pp. 169–217.

——— and William Landes, eds. 1974. *Essays in the Economics of Crime and Punishment* (New York, Columbia University Press).

Bilder, Richard B. 1974. "The Emerging Right of Physical Enforcement of Fisheries Measures Beyond Territorial Limits," University of Wisconsin Sea Grant College Program, Technical Report #22.

Black, Cyril E., Richard A. Falk, Klaus E. Knorr, and Oran R. Young. 1968. *Neutralization and World Politics* (Princeton, Princeton University Press).

Brierly, J.L. 1932. "Sanctions," *Problems of Peace and War,* vol. 17, pp. 67–84.

———. 1963. *The Law of Nations* 6th ed. (New York, Oxford University Press).

Bronfenbrenner, Urie. 1970. *Two Worlds of Childhood* (New York, Russell Sage Foundation).

Buchanan, James M. 1962. "Politics, Policy and the Pigovian Margins," *Economica,* n.s. 29, pp. 17–28.

————. 1965. "An Economic Theory of Clubs," *Economica,* n.s. 32, pp. 1–14.

————. 1968. *The Demand and Supply of Public Goods* (Chicago, Rand Mc-Nally).

————. 1975. *The Limits of Liberty* (Chicago, University of Chicago Press).

———— and Gordon Tullock. 1962. *The Calculus of Consent* (Ann Arbor, University of Michigan Press).

Buck, Eugene H. 1973. "National Patterns and Trends of Fishery Development in the North Pacific," *Alaska and the Law of the Sea* (Anchorage, Arctic Environmental Information and Data Center).

Bull, Hedley. 1977. *The Anarchical Society* (New York, Columbia University Press).

Burke, William T., Richard Legatski, and William W. Woodhead. 1975. *National and International Law Enforcement in the Ocean* (Seattle, University of Washington Press).

Calabresi, Guido. 1972. "Transaction Costs, Resource Allocation, and Liability Rules," pp. 194–201 in Robert Dorfman and Nancy S. Dorfman, eds., *Economics of the Environment* (New York, Norton).

Cartwright, Dorwin and Alvin Zander, eds. 1968. *Group Dynamics* 3rd ed. (New York, Harper & Row).

Chayes, Abram. 1972. "An Enquiry into the Workings of Arms Control Agreements," *Harvard Law Review,* vol. 85, pp. 905–969.

Chitwood, Philip E. 1969. "Japanese, Soviet, and South Korean Fisheries off Alaska," *United States Fish and Wildlife Circular 310,* United States Department of the Interior (Washington, GPO).

Christy, Francis T., Jr. and Anthony C. Scott. 1965. *The Commonwealth in Ocean Fisheries* (Baltimore, Johns Hopkins University Press).

Coase, Ronald. 1960. "The Problem of Social Cost," *Journal of Law and Economics,* vol. 3, pp. 1–44.

Copes, Parzival. 1976. "The Law of the Sea and Management of Anadromous Fish Stocks," Discussion Paper 76-11-1, Simon Fraser University.

Dahl, Robert A. 1956. *A Preface to Democratic Theory* (Chicago, University of Chicago Press).

Dales, J. H. 1968. *Pollution, Property, and Prices* (Toronto, University of Toronto Press).

Davis, Otto A. and Morton I. Kamien. 1969. "Externalities, Information and Alternative Collective Action," in *The Analysis and Evaluation of Public Expenditures: The PPB System* (Vol. I) (Washington, GPO), pp. 67–86.

Dorfman, Robert and Nancy S. Dorfman, eds. 1972. *Economics of the Environment* (New York, Norton).

Downs, Anthony. 1957. *An Economic Theory of Democracy* (New York, Harper & Row).

————. 1967. *Inside Bureaucracy* (Boston, Little Brown).

Doxey, Margaret P. 1971. *Economic Sanctions and International Enforcement* (London, Oxford University Press).

Dworkin, Ronald. 1967. "The Model of Rules," *University of Chicago Law Review,* vol. 35, pp. 14–46.

————. 1978. *Taking Rights Seriously* (Cambridge, Harvard University Press).

Eckert, Ross D. 1975. "Exploitation of Deep Ocean Minerals: Regulatory Mechanisms and United States Policy," *Journal of Law and Economics,* vol. 17, pp. 143–177.

Edwards, Ward and Amos Tversky, eds. 1967. *Decision Making* (Harmondsworth, Penguin).

Emberg, Truman, 1977. "Western Alaska Salmon and Article 55," Western Alaska Cooperative Marketing Association, xeroxed.

Emmet, Dorothy. 1972. *Function, Purpose and Powers* (London, Temple University Press).

Falk, Richard A. 1964. "Janus Tormented: The International Law of Internal War," in James N. Rosenau, ed. *International Aspects of Civil Strife* (Princeton, Princeton University Press), pp. 185–248.

———. 1966. "On the Quasi-Legislative Competence of the General Assembly," *American Journal of International Law,* vol. 60, pp. 782–791.

———. 1970. *The Status of Law in International Society* (Princeton, Princeton University Press).

——— and Richard Barnet, eds. 1965. *Security in Disarmament* (Princeton, Princeton University Press).

Fisher, Bart S. 1971. "Enforcing Export Quota Agreements: The Case of Coffee," *Harvard International Law Journal,* vol. 12, pp. 401–435.

Fisher, Roger. 1969. *International Conflict for Beginners* (New York, Harper and Row).

Frohlich, Norman. 1974. "Self-Interest or Altruism: What Difference?" *Journal of Conflict Resolution,* vol. XVIII, pp. 55–73.

——— and Joe A. Oppenheimer. 1970. "I Get By with a Little Help from my Friends," *World Politics,* vol. XVIII, pp. 104–120.

———, Joe A. Oppenheimer, and Oran R. Young. 1971. *Political Leadership and Collective Goods* (Princeton, Princeton University Press).

——— and Joe A. Oppenheimer. 1971. *An Entrepreneurial Theory of Politics.* Ph.D. Dissertation, Princeton University.

——— and Joe A. Oppenheimer. 1974. "The Carrot and the Stick: Optimal Program Mixes for Entrepreneurial Political Leaders," *Public Choice,* vol. XIX, pp. 43–61.

——— and Joe A. Oppenheimer. 1978. *Modern Political Economy* (Englewood Cliffs, Prentice Hall).

Fuller, Lon L. 1958. "Positivism and Fidelity to Law: A Reply to Professor Hart," *Harvard Law Review,* vol. 71, pp. 630–671.

———. 1969. *The Morality of Law* rev. ed. (New Haven: Yale University Press).

Furubotn, Eirik and Svetozar Pejovich. 1972. "Property Rights and Economic Theory: A Survey of Recent Literature," *Journal of Economic Literature,* vol. X, pp. 1137–1162.

Gergen, Kenneth J. 1969. *The Psychology of Behavior Exchange* (Reading, Addison Wesley).

Gerth, H. H. and C. Wright Mills, eds., 1958. *From Max Weber: Essays in Sociology* (New York: Oxford University Press).

Gillette, Robert. 1974. "Nuclear Testing Violations: Keeping It All in the Family," *Science,* vol. 185, pp. 506–510.

Glasser, Daniel. 1972. *Adult Crime and Social Policy* (Englewood Cliffs, Prentice Hall).

Goffman, Erving. 1971. *Relations in Public* (New York, Basic Books).

Gordon, H. Scott. 1954. "The Economic Theory of A Common Property Resource: The Fishery," *Journal of Political Economy*, vol. 62, pp. 124–142.

Goulding, M. P., ed. 1966. *The Nature of Law: Readings in Legal Philosophy* (New York: Random House).

Guerin, Daniel. 1970. *Anarchism: From Theory to Practice* (New York, Monthly Review Press).

Gulland, J. A., ed. 1972. *The Fish Resources of the Ocean* (London, Fishing News (Books)).

Haas, Ernst. 1958. *The Uniting of Europe* (Stanford, Stanford University Press).

Haig-Brown, Roderick L. 1967. "Canada's Pacific Salmon," Information and Consumer Service, Department of Fisheries of Canada.

Hart, H.L.A. 1958. "Positivism and the Separation of Law and Morals," *Harvard Law Review*, vol. 71, pp. 593–629.

———. 1961. *The Concept of Law* (Oxford, Oxford University Press).

Hart, Jeffrey. 1976. "Three Approaches to the Measurement of Power in International Relations," *International Organization*, vol. 30, pp. 289–305.

Head, John G. 1974. *Public Goods and Public Welfare* (Durham, Duke University Press).

Hempel, Carl G. 1965. *Aspects of Scientific Explanation* (New York, Free Press).

———. 1966. *Philosophy of Natural Science* (Englewood Cliffs, Prentice Hall).

Henderson, J.M. and R.E. Quandt. 1958. *Microeconomic Theory* (New York, McGraw Hill).

Henkin, Louis. 1968. *How Nations Behave* (New York, Praeger).

Hoag, Stephen H. and Robert R. French. 1976. "The Incidental Catch of Halibut by Foreign Trawlers," Seattle, IPHC Scientific Report No. 60.

Hobbes, Thomas. 1962. *Leviathan,* original date 1651 (New York, Macmillan).

Hoebel, E. Adamson. 1954. *The Law of Primitive Man* (Cambridge, Harvard University Press).

Janis, Irving L. 1972. *Victims of Groupthink* (Boston, Houghton Mifflin).

de Jouvenel, Bertrand. 1963. *The Pure Theory of Politics* (New Haven, Yale University Press).

Kaplan, Morton and Nicholas deB. Katzenbach. 1961. *The Political Foundations of International Law* (New York, Wiley).

Kapp, K. William. 1950. *The Social Costs of Private Enterprise* (Cambridge, Harvard University Press).

Keohane, Robert O. and Joseph S. Nye. 1977. *Power and Interdependence* (Boston, Little Brown).

Kiesler, C.A. and Sara B. Kiesler. 1969. *Conformity* (Reading, Addison Wesley).

Koers, Albert W. 1973. *International Regulation of Marine Fisheries* (London, Fishing News (Books)).

Larkin, P.A. 1977. "An Epitaph for the Concept of Maximum Sustained Yield," *Transactions of the American Fisheries Society*, vol. 106, pp. 1–11.

Lasswell, Harold and Abraham Kaplan. 1950. *Power and Society* (New Haven, Yale University Press).

Levy, Marion J. 1972. *Modernization: Latecomers and Survivors* (New York, Basic Books).

Lewis, David K. 1969. *Convention: A Philosophical Study* (Cambridge, Harvard University Press).

Locke, John. 1952. *Second Treatise on Civil Government,* original date 1689 (Indianapolis, Bobbs-Merrill).

Luce, R. Duncan and Howard Raiffa. 1957. *Games and Decisions* (New York, Wiley).

Mair, Lucy. 1962. *Primitive Government* (Harmondsworth: Penguin).

Malinowski, Bronislaw. 1926. *Crime and Custom in Savage Society* (New York, Harcourt Brace).

March, James G. and Herbert A. Simon. 1958. *Organizations* (New York, Wiley).

McDougal, Myres S. and Associates. 1960. *Studies in World Public Order* (New Haven, Yale University Press).

McDougal, Myres S., Harold D. Lasswell, and James C. Miller. 1967. *The Interpretation of Agreements and World Public Order* (New Haven, Yale University Press).

McKean, Roland. 1965. "The Unseen Hand in Government," *American Economic Review,* vol. LV, pp. 496–506.

————. 1974. "Economics of Ethical and Behavioral Codes," mimeographed.

McNamara, Robert. 1963. "McNamara Statement to Senate Committee on Test Ban," Washington, *United States Information Service* (14 August 1963).

Mendlovitz, Saul H., ed. 1975. *On the Creation of a Just World Order* (New York, Free Press).

Middlemiss, D.W. 1976. "Canadian Maritime Enforcement Policies," xeroxed manuscript.

Mishan, E. J. 1967. *The Costs of Economic Growth* (Harmondsworth, Penguin).

————. 1971. "The Postwar Literature on Externalities: An Interpretive Essay," *Journal of Economic Literature,* vol. IX, pp. 1–28.

Naab, Ronald C. 1969. "The Role of International Agreements in Alaskan Fisheries," *Commercial Fisheries Review,* vol. 30, pp. 46–56.

National Marine Fisheries Service, Law Enforcement Division (Juneau). 1976. "Violation of International Agreements by Foreign Vessels off Alaska, 1961–Present." 21 September.

Neustadt, Richard. 1970. *Alliance Politics* (New York, Columbia University Press).

Nicholas, H.G. 1962. *The United Nations as a Political Institution* 2nd ed. (London, Oxford University Press).

Niskanen, William A. 1971. *Bureaucracy and Representative Government* (Chicago, Aldine Atherton).

Nozick, Robert. 1974. *Anarchy, State, and Utopia* (New York, Basic Books).

Oliver, Edward F. 1971. "Wet War—North Pacific," *San Diego Law Review,* vol. 8, pp. 621–638.

Olson, Mancur, Jr. 1965. *The Logic of Collective Action* (Cambridge, Harvard University Press).

Onuf, Nicholas G. 1974. "Law-Making in the Global Community: A Working Paper," mimeographed, Princeton.

Page, Alfred N., ed. 1968. *Utility Theory: A Book of Readings* (New York, Wiley).

Pennock, J. Roland and John W. Chapman, eds. 1970. *Political and Legal Obligation (Nomos XII)* (New York, Atherton).

Pigou, A. C. 1932. *The Economics of Welfare,* 4th ed. (London, Macmillan).

Pitkin, Hanna. 1965. "Obligation and Consent—I," *American Political Science Review,* vol. LIX, pp. 990–999.

———. 1966. "Obligation and Consent—II," *American Political Science Review,* vol. LX, pp. 39–52.

Quinton, Anthony, ed. 1967. *Political Philosophy* (London, Oxford University Press).

Randall, Alan. 1974. "Coase Externality Theory in a Policy Context," *Natural Resources Journal,* vol. 14, pp. 35–54.

Rapoport, Anatol. 1964. *Strategy and Conscience* (New York, Harper & Row).

——— and Albert M. Chammah. 1965. *Prisoner's Dilemma* (Ann Arbor, University of Michigan Press).

Rawls, John. 1955. "Two Concepts of Rules," *Philosophical Review,* vol. 64, pp. 3–32.

———. 1971. *A Theory of Justice* (Cambridge, Harvard University Press).

Reich, Charles A. 1964. "The New Property," *Yale Law Journal,* vol. 73, pp. 733–787.

Reisman, W. Michael. 1971. "Sanctions and Enforcement," in Cyril E. Black and Richard A. Falk, eds. *The Future of the International Legal Order* (vol. III: *Conflict Management*) (Princeton, Princeton University Press), pp. 273–335.

Riesman, David. 1950. *The Lonely Crowd* (New Haven, Yale University Press).

Riker, William and Peter Ordeshook. 1973. *An Introduction to Positive Political Theory* (Englewood Cliffs, Prentice Hall).

Robinson, Timothy S. 1977. "Study Shows Few of D.C. Offenders Convicted, Jailed," *Washington Post,* 23 January, pp. B1–2.

Rosenne, Shabtai. 1973. *The World Court* 3rd rev. ed. (Dobbs Ferry, N.Y., Oceana).

Rothenberg, Jerome. 1961. *The Measurement of Social Welfare* (Englewood Cliffs, Prentice Hall).

Rottenberg, Simon, ed. 1973. *The Economics of Crime and Punishment* (Washington, American Enterprise Institute for Public Policy Research).

Schapera, I. 1967. *Government and Politics in Tribal Societies* (New York, Shocken Books).

Schelling, Thomas C. 1960. *The Strategy of Conflict* (Cambridge, Harvard University Press).

———. 1966. *Arms and Influence* (New Haven, Yale University Press).

——— and Morton H. Halperin. 1961. *Strategy and Arms Control* (New York, Twentieth Century Fund).

Scitovsky, T. 1943. "A Note on Profit Maximization and its Implications," *Review of Economics and Statistics,* vol. XI, pp. 57–60.

Scott, Anthony. 1973. *Natural Resources: The Economics of Conservation* (Toronto, McClelland and Stewart).

Shatz, Marshall, ed. 1971. *The Essential Works of Anarchism* (New York, Bantam Books).

Simon, Herbert A. 1959. "Theories of Decision Making in Economics and Behavioral Science," *American Economic Review,* vol. XLIX, pp. 253–283.

Skud, Bernard E. 1976. "Jurisdictional and Administrative Limitations Affecting Management of the Halibut Fishery." IPHC Scientific Report No. 59, Seattle.

Staaf, Robert and Francis Tannian. 1973. *Externalities: Theoretical Dimensions of Political Economy* (Port Washington, N.Y., Kennikat Press).

Steinbruner, John. 1974. *The Cybernetic Theory of Decision* (Princeton, Princeton University Press).

Stigler, George. 1970. "The Optimum Enforcement of Laws," *Journal of Political Economy,* vol. 78, pp. 526–536.

Stockholm International Peace Research Institute. (Annual). *World Armaments and Disarmament* (Stockholm, Almquist and Wicksell).

———. 1973. *Ten Years of the Partial Test Ban Treaty, 1963–1973.* Research Report No. 11, August.

Stoessinger, John G. and Associates. 1964. *Financing the United Nations System* (Washington, Brookings).

Tauber, Ronald S. 1969. "Enforcement of IATA Agreements," *Harvard International Law Journal,* vol. 10, pp. 1–33.

Taylor, Michael. 1976. *Anarchy and Cooperation* (London, Wiley).

Taylor, Telford. 1970a. *Guilt, Responsibility and the Third Reich* (Cambridge, Heffer).

———. 1970b. *Nuremberg and Vietnam* (Chicago, Quadrangle Books).

Thibaut, John W. and Harold W. Kelley. 1959. *The Social Psychology of Groups* (New York, Wiley).

Tullock, Gordon. 1965. *The Politics of Bureaucracy* (Washington, Public Affairs Press).

———. 1974. "Does Punishment Deter Crime?" *The Public Interest,* vol. 36, pp. 103–111.

Tversky, Amos and Daniel Kahneman. 1974. "Judgment under Uncertainty: Heuristics and Biases," *Science,* vol. 185, pp. 1124–1131.

Wilimovsky, Norman J. 1976. "Obtaining Protein from the Oceans: Opportunities and Constraints," *Transactions of the 41st North American Wildlife and Natural Resources Conference,* Washington, pp. 58–78.

Wittgenstein, Ludwig. 1953. *Philosophical Investigations* (New York, Macmillan).

von Wright, G. H. 1963. *Norms and Action* (New York, Humanities Press).

Wylie, Laurence. 1974. *Village in the Vaucluse* 3rd ed. (Cambridge, Harvard University Press).

Yale Law Journal. 1973. "New Perspectives on International Environmental Law," vol. 82, pp. 1659–1680.

York, Herbert F., ed. 1973. *Arms Control: Readings from Scientific American* (San Francisco, Freeman).

Young, Oran R. 1969. "Interdependencies in World Politics," *International Journal,* vol. XXIV, pp. 726–750.

————. 1972. "The Actors in World Politics," in James N. Rosenau, Vincent Davis, and Maurice East, eds. *The Analysis of International Politics* (New York, Free Press), pp. 125–143.

————. 1975. *Bargaining: Formal Theories of Negotiation* (Urbana, University of Illinois Press).

————. 1978. "Anarchy and Social Choice: Reflections on the International Polity," *World Politics,* vol. XXXI, pp. 241–263.

Zartman, I. William, ed. 1976. *The 50% Solution* (Garden City, Doubleday).

Zeckhauser, Richard and Elmer Shaefer. 1968. "Public Policy and Normative Economic Theory," in Raymond A. Bauer and Kenneth J. Gergen, eds. *The Study of Policy Formation* (New York, Free Press), pp. 27–101.

Name index*

* The letter *n* following a page number refers to material contained in a footnote.

Subject index*

* The letter *n* following a page number refers to material contained in a footnote. The abbreviation INPFC stands for International North Pacific Fisheries Convention; PTB for Partial Nuclear Test Ban Treaty. These abbreviations follow the usage in the text.